Sales on a Beermat

. ...ke   ... ...eermat.biz,   ...ch helps
entrepreneurs and fast-growing companies around the world.
He is a Visiting Fellow in Enterprise and Entrepreneurship at
London South Bank University, and a Fellow of the
Professional Speakers Association. He writes a weekly column
'My Business' for the *Financial Times* every Saturday.

Mike co-founded The Instruction Set in 1984, which grew
to 150 people in 5 years before being sold to Hoskyns Group.
He was responsible for all sales and marketing. He has since
been involved in 17 start-ups. In 2002 he co-authored the
bestselling *The Beermat Entrepreneur*. He can be contacted at
mike@beermat.biz

Chris West is a professional writer, with a background in
marketing and PR. He has written fiction and books on
business, personal development, writing good English and
travel. He is co-author of *The Beermat Entrepreneur* and of the
other *Beermat* guides, and sole author of *Marketing on a Beermat*.

Praise for *Sales on a Beermat*

'Highly entertaining, original, and full of practical and concise tips.'
Iain Henderson, partner, Accenture

'Mike is the Father Ted of sales: irreverent, endearing and wonderfully effective. Generating more sales isn't a mystery anymore – Mike has the wonderful ability to make the complex clear. Wake up the sales person within you with Mike's obscenely simple concepts.'
Matt Drought, director, The Natural Training Company Ltd

'A truly sizzling read, guaranteed to improve your technique for seduction and sales alike – I couldn't put it down.' **Gavin Johnson, director of strategy and interaction, Schmakk**

'In professional partnerships we like to think we don't have to sell. This is a dangerous illusion – luckily this book is here to show us how, and why it needn't be hell. Inspiring and motivational.' **John Beevor, commercial lawyer, BPE Solicitors**

'Mike and Chris's books are acquiring a reputation for readability and entertainment, but also for having a lot to say. *Sales on a Beermat* carries on a fast-growing tradition.' **Lucy Armstrong, chief executive, The Alchemists**

'We have just been engaged by an international bank to implement a new software system which could mean upwards of £500k of revenue – all from one technique in this book!' **Nigel Winship, founder, First Thought Consulting**

'The day of the stand-alone salesman is over. This book enables everyone to understand how they can assist in revenue generation.' **Graeme Finch, chief executive, Business Link Milton Keynes, Oxon & Bucks**

'Mike and Chris demystify the sales process and prove that professional sales and negotiation skills can be taught and learned.' **Sean Derrig, national franchise manager, Snap-on Tools**

'*Sales on a Beermat* does exactly what it claims – it helped double our sales in three months.' **Stefan Foster, managing director, National Computing Centre**

Sales on a
Beermat

Mike Southon
&
Chris West

rh

BUSINESS
BOOKS

To our fathers: Ken Southon, a great salesman,
and Tony West, a great lover of the English language,
with thanks for all they taught us

Published by Random House Business Books 2008

4 6 8 10 9 7 5 3

First published in Great Britain in 2005 by
Random House Business Books

This edition published in Great Britain in 2008 by
Random House Business Books
Random House, 20 Vauxhall Bridge Road,
London SW1V 2SA

www.randomhouse.co.uk

Addresses for companies within The Random House Group Limited can be found at:
www.randomhouse.co.uk/offices.htm

The Random House Group Limited Reg. No. 954009

A CIP catalogue record for this book
is available from the British Library

ISBN 9781847940063

The Random House Group Limited supports The Forest Stewardship
Council (FSC®), the leading international forest certification organisation.
Our books carrying the FSC label are printed on FSC® certified paper.
FSC is the only forest certification scheme endorsed by the leading
environmental organisations, including Greenpeace. Our
paper procurement policy can be found at
www.randomhouse.co.uk/environment

MIX
Paper from
responsible sources
FSC® C016897

Typeset in Foundry Form Sans and Bembo
Design and make-up by Roger Walker
Printed in Great Britain by Clays Ltd, St Ives plc

Foreword

by Stephen Fry

Sales! Ghastly people with loud clothes and louder aftershave, ruining your day by trying to sell you stuff you don't want and certainly don't need…

If this is you, please put this book down immediately. This book is written by nice people for nice people.

Mike Southon and Chris West helped entrepreneurs with *The Beermat Entrepreneur* and corporate types with *The Boardroom Entrepreneur*. And now they're here to help you and me.

I say 'you and me' because Robert Louis Stevenson was right. We all have to sell something to survive. Mike and Chris explain how to do this without upsetting your friends, alienating your customers or losing your professional dignity.

This is a sales book for everyone: lawyers, accountants, software engineers, managers, anyone starting out on their own in business. Even actors and writers have much to learn from it; more, perhaps, than many of us would care to admit. Luckily, that learning should be easy, as the book is written with clarity and wit.

Be nice; be yourself; sell the 'Beermat' way; enjoy the experience and enjoy this book.

Stephen Fry, Writer, Performer, Director

'Everybody makes a living by selling something.'

Robert Louis Stevenson

Contents

Note from Mike

Like all Beermat books, this has been a team effort. It is written in the first person because it is at the same time a very personal one: selling has been my life for a quarter of a century. This is my story.

But a story only becomes literature in the hands of an author – this is the exceptional talent of Chris West, who has observed with the novelist's eye my sales efforts over the years, even before I was officially in a sales role. Chris has turned this havoc into a clear and logical model, as he did with *The Beermat Entrepreneur* and *The Boardroom Entrepreneur*.

It is based on my 'Sales on a Beermat' talk, which I have given to audiences around the world. The talk attracts all kinds of business people: entrepreneurs, replacement windows sales-people, computer scientists, senior lawyers and even managing directors. We make no apology for casting the net as wide when considering the audience for this book, as all the different kinds of business person seem to benefit from what we say.

This book would not have been possible without my favourite customers and employers over the years: Sid Fox (ICL), Ricky Gervais (University of London Union), Sam Shrouder (Apollo Leisure), Phil Tee (RiverSoft), Jamie Mitchell (e-start), Phil Smith (Cisco Systems), Rachael Stock (Pearson Education), Sir John Rose (Rolls-Royce), Leslie Stretch (Sun Microsystems),

Ian Henderson (Accenture), Harry Drnec (Red Bull) and of course Clare Smith (Random House).

My personal learning process never ends, so special mention to Thomas Power, who has shown me how to *network*, Harold Chee who has taught me about *guanxi*, and my wife Virginia and son James who keep trying to teach me how to *listen*.

And very special thanks to our old friend Graham Michelli, who saw an early draft and with his expert marketer's eye asked, 'Who is this book written *for*?'

A very good question! I hope we have provided a good answer.

London 2005

I'm standing in front of an audience of aspiring entrepreneurs. Not just any audience: this is the entrepreneurship class at a major international business school; the people I'm talking to have come from all over the world, and paid a great deal of money, to become the best businessmen and women they can. They are practitioners, too – the school doesn't accept raw graduates but insists on real work experience.

To be honest, I'm a bit overawed. But I get on with my talk on the Beermat enterprise. I get to the point where I stress the importance of sales in the start-up. Heads nod. Of course they do: these bright individuals know as well as I do that

no sales = no revenue = no business.

On an impulse, I ask how many of them have been on sales training. I assume most of them will have been, but I'm interested to know the exact breakdown. Seventy per cent? Sixty?

An uneasy silence settles.

Not a single hand goes up.

'Nobody?' I ask jokily. This is a wind-up. Someone will crack any moment, and say of course they've done sales training, now can you get on with your talk please, Mike.

But instead, they all look nervously at one another, and start shaking their heads.

I suddenly realise they mean it. Not one of these aspiring Masters of the Business Universe has made any formal study of the most basic business skill of all – selling.

I ask why, and get three kinds of answer. Some 'just haven't thought about it'. Others say they are more interested in strategy: someone else will go out on the road and actually sell the stuff. A third group say they understand this is a gap in their knowledge, but they are not 'sales types' – it takes a certain type of person to sell… I'm horrified – but resolve to go away and get this book written.

Looking back, I hope that after my talk the 'just haven't thought about it' ones did think about sales, hard. I hope the aspiring strategists did too, unless they wanted to end up with businesses like those in the late Nineties that ate capital, churned out business plans, sold nothing and went broke. The ones who considered they weren't sales types had a much better point – but that simply meant they should not become full-time sales people, not that they should be totally ignorant about, and divorced from, the revenue-winning process. I assume they studied the basics of finance, even though they were not planning to become accountants.

Next day, Chris and I were doing one-on-one coaching sessions with working entrepreneurs. Some were sole traders, others had teams assembled. Some were just starting out, others had been in business a while. Their problems, as you can imagine, varied, but a theme running through our conversations was lack of revenue. They all had good ideas, most had some customers, hardly any had as many customers as they needed, none of them was using their customer relationships as effectively as they should. In other words, they weren't selling properly.

My resolve to write this book grew stronger.

The truth is that *everybody* in business, or in any kind of service where there is a whiff of competition – the case for much of the modern public sector – has to sell. This is, of course, particularly true in start-ups. But it's also the case in established small and medium-sized enterprises and in large organisations that have decided to innovate their way out of stagnation. It's true in franchises: even if the franchisor promises to provide leads, franchisees still have to use sales skills to turn those leads into repeat business (the good franchisees will be busy creating their own leads, as well). It is painfully true in professional partnerships, where brilliant practitioners find themselves losing out in the race to the top, suddenly less important than competent peers 'who can bring in business'.

Let's face it: it's true everywhere. So let's give it the status of a scientific law, and name it after the great Scot we quoted at the start of this book. Stevenson's Law:

Everybody has to sell

If Stevenson's Law fills you with horror, please don't put this book down. Let me put it another way...

Every organisation needs at least one front-line salesperson. Everybody else in the organisation must understand how the sales process works, and must play a part, however small, in that process

Does that make you feel better?

It should – because the message does not have to be a scary one. This book will explain the sales process, the roles that everyone has in it (front-line or support), how to select people for those roles and how everyone can fulfil their role to the best of his or her ability.

The process and roles are remarkably similar for all sizes of business – the main difference between the tiny business and the giant is that in the former you have to double up roles. The self-employed sole trader, of course, has to do them all…

If this is beginning to sound scary again, relax. The answers are in here. I know, because I've been giving this advice for years, and hundreds of people have told me it has made a huge difference to their careers and/or businesses.

Many of them have even said they ended up finding their selling roles fun!

Chapter One: Sales and the Beermat Context

Our books *The Beermat Entrepreneur* and *The Boardroom Entrepreneur* set out a model of business development. This book is based on this model. In this chapter I shall briefly restate it and expand a little on those aspects particularly relevant to sales.

The Beermat enterprise usually starts with an entrepreneur and one or two friends – often in a pub and sometimes without paper handy, so the great business idea has to be planned on the back of a beermat. It is helpful if one of these individuals is a sales person – but if not, the team shouldn't worry, just start looking for a salesperson at once (there will be plenty of material in this book to help them find one).

There are three things they must define at once.

First is the *elevator pitch* – a brief summary of exactly what it is they intend to do, for whom, and why customers should buy it from them rather than from someone else. Time spent honing the elevator pitch is time well spent. A good starting point is the *magic question*: 'Where's the pain?' Where are customers incurring cost, waste and inefficiency? Where are they missing opportunities, getting lousy service, having to search hard for information, losing their own customers (etc)?

Next is the *mentor* for the business, a senior and respected business person who will give advice and open doors. This person may well be responsible for getting you the third essential on your beermat...

...Your *first customer*. The Beermat methodology was developed in horrified response to the dotcom era notion of throwing money at clever-sounding ideas then finally seeing if anyone actually wanted to buy the product. We say that start-ups should have a real customer in mind from Day One, and be speaking to this person – and it must always be a person; a company name isn't good enough – as soon as possible. This is why they need a sales specialist fast: if they do not have one, it will probably fall to the entrepreneur to make initial contacts. The entrepreneur will be happy to do this, and probably good at it, but is usually not the right person to build the relationship over the long term or to negotiate and close actual deals.

It is already apparent that for the idea to succeed, a team is needed. A *balanced business team* comprises specialists in the core areas of business:

★ sales

★ finance

★ innovation

★ delivery (making the innovator's ideas actually work repeatably and reliably)

Note that we say 'sales', not marketing. The strategic 'who are we selling to?' aspects of marketing should be understood at the start and encapsulated in the elevator pitch. Once that has been sorted, the start-up needs relationships with actual customers, and these are best created and sustained by good salespeople. Marketers who have the sales instinct are, of course, ideal for this job, but they should call it sales and do so with pride.

The members of this team are called the *cornerstones* of the business: the entrepreneur is the apex, but the success of the enterprise is built on the cornerstones' commitment and ability. As such, they should be given real influence over and serious stakes in that success.

Once the business has its first paying customer, it works with the customer to write a White Paper. What was it like for the customer? How did they actually use the product? What did they find particularly helpful? What did they dislike or end up not using? How could it be improved? This will help the business refine the product, as well as the elevator pitch and its understanding of the real market it is in. The sales cornerstone will oversee the writing of this paper, getting input from technical and financial specialists. He or she will also use it, in a repackaged form, as a sales document.

The start-up should go through the White Paper process with the first few customers, until the team has a clear idea of the 'shape' of the market. This virtuous circle of product development and market discovery can only be done via excellent relationships with customers – with human beings, not organisations – and (forgive me for labouring the point but it is so important) this is best done by someone with sales skills and the sales personality.

The business should now be growing. Up to the point where it is the entrepreneur and four cornerstones, plus maybe an office manager/receptionist, it is in its *seedling* phase. Bright people are then required to form the 'Dream Team', the next level of people taken on board. These must be positive, team-spirited doers. As it takes these people on, the business enters its next phase, the *sapling*: the core products and their markets are well-understood; it's time to get out there and sell as many of the right products to the right customers as possible.

The sales cornerstone will take on sales staff, and have to do some sales management. However he or she should still spend most of their time looking for new business.

When the headcount gets to about twenty or thirty people, the sapling enterprise will change culturally. Up to now it has been a tribe: it is about to become a small organisation. It has to decide if it wants to stay tribal – a twenty-five person 'boutique', often a pleasant and highly profitable way to do business – or to really get its head down and go for growth. The cultural consequences of choosing the latter option are massive. It will never be quite as much fun, but the business can grow fast and build up a substantial capital value.

If it makes the leap across this cultural gap and pursues growth, the business becomes a proper tree. Up to about one hundred and fifty people, it is a *young tree*. During the young-tree phase, full-blown systems have to be set up, and the entrepreneur and cornerstones have to consider their own roles: they may now be burnt out and/or getting in the way. The sales cornerstone may well find themselves managing sales full-time – not usually their favourite activity. Better to employ a sales manager and get the cornerstone back out on the road, talking to potential large new customers.

The sales methodologies outlined in Chapters Eight and Nine are particularly appropriate for these businesses.

Beyond a hundred and fifty people, we have a *Mighty Oak*, a substantial, structured organisation.

The story is not over, of course: the oak (to keep the metaphor going) is in a highly competitive forest, with other trees seeking to take its light and nutrition. It needs to keep in contact with its customers – the Beermat ideal – and not become too inward-looking. The moment when internal processes become more important than happy customers is the moment when the next phase in the cycle – *decay* – sets in.

Throughout the entire journey, the salespeople should have been the principal (but not only) 'eyes and ears' of the company, always alert for customer pain.

Two other points about the Beermat methodology...

Beermat businesses *fund from revenue*. Even if they are in a capital-intensive area, they strive to do this by all means possible. Hence, of course, the centrality of sales (= revenue generation) activity at all times in the life of the business.

There are two main reasons why we say this. One is that the search for capital can be draining, at a time when the business needs to be concentrating on customer pain and its solution. A 'fund from revenue' mindset prevents the business from getting stuck in this grisly mire – and ironically can make capital easier to come by. Lenders want to lend to people who can clearly stand on their own feet.

The other is that the relationship between capital providers and entrepreneurs is often a fraught one. Hopefully this will be less so when our next Beermat Guide, *Finance on a Beermat*, comes out – but even then, cracks will no doubt appear.

We also expressed a *philosophy of business*. It's about creating long-term value for yourself, your people and your customers: 'win-win situations', to use the jargon. Beermat enterprises are ethical, fair and, very important, fun to work in. They make money – lots of it – by providing customers with what they need in a way that is profitable.

Sales in the Beermat company follow this philosophy. Beermat salespeople are honest, genuinely care about customers and enjoy their work.

From the above, it can be seen that the Beermat model isn't just for start-ups. Many SMEs are in the 'young tree' phase; and much of the material in this book is applicable to, and has been used by, large companies, including some of the mightiest oaks on the UK corporate landscape! Professional partnerships and 'sole trader' – one-person – businesses also need to sell in the Beermat fashion – there are special Appendices for them at the end of the book.

beermat salespeople are **honest**, genuinely **care about customers** and **enjoy their work**

Chapter Two: # The Natural Salesperson

The Beermat Entrepreneur began with a discussion on the character of entrepreneurs; I'd like to continue the tradition by taking an early look at 'natural' salespeople. Do they exist, and if so, what kind of people are they?

Do they exist?

Oh, yes. I can spot them in crowds, no doubt because I'm one myself. So was my dad, who sold British Leyland cars to Eastern Europe. My grandfather was a 'sales natural', too: the Reverend Arthur E. Southon was a missionary in China and Nigeria (and even wrote a book about his experiences...)

What kind of people are they?

Almost every book on sales lists character traits for salespeople – ambition, persistence, intelligence, self-belief, the ability to listen, a skin as tough as a rhinoceros in a suit of armour (and so on). I accept all of these, but believe there is one key to selling that trumps them all. That is simply to be *liked*.

Of course, we all have friends, so we are all liked. But most of us have a reasonably small, close circle of real friends plus a wider range of acquaintances, and prefer it that way. Natural salespeople possess a slightly different and particular way of being liked. If you went to college, think back to who was always at the bar, buying drinks? Who got things organised – societies, pub evenings, outings to gigs or clubs? At a party, now, who chats to lots of people during the evening? Who is always eager to make new acquaintances? Who's always enthusing about new projects?

Back in the eighteenth century, Dr Johnson called such individuals 'clubbable'. Modern writers refer to them as 'social magnets' (Professor Richard Wiseman in *The Luck Factor*) or 'persuaders' (Malcolm Gladwell in *The Tipping Point*). They are the master networkers (or, to use the jargon, the 'network nodes'). In both Dr Johnson's era and our own – and in all of human history, in my guess – they kept society alive and fun: without them, life would grind to a sullen, inward-looking halt.

Why are they liked so much?

They have great *charm*. I have been at social gatherings where certain celebrities and politicians have 'worked' rooms, winning over a large number of people via a series of brief but memorable one-to-one encounters. It's hugely impressive to watch, and to experience. You do not feel you have been conned; you simply feel the person has something special about them.

Studies show that such individuals use *naturally positive body language*: they smile more; they make more eye contact (but not too much); they adopt an open posture rather than a defensive one when talking to people. And they do all this instinctively, not because they have read books or been on courses telling them to do so.

Many also have excellent *memories*. Carole Stone runs a wonderful network of thousands of people up and down the UK, of which I am lucky to be one. When I call her up, she remembers who I am, some facts about me and even conversations we have had in the past. Most people just can't do that – anthropologists have worked out that beyond about one hundred and fifty people most of us begin to conflate and confuse individuals.

Mercifully, you don't have to have Carole's memory to be a great salesperson. It certainly helps, though; and if you don't have it, make sure you have a good back-up system that makes it look as if you have.

More important than all of the above, however, is simply that the natural salesperson *likes people*. Networkers network because they enjoy it, because they get pleasure from meeting people, from making new friends and from 'making things happen' socially. Will Rogers, who 'never met a man he didn't like', was a sales natural (and was a very successful salesman, for himself).

Naturally, such people are liked back.

There is a potential downside to 'social magnets': the butterfly. You know the type. They're your best mate for the five minutes they're with you; contact them a few weeks later and it's, 'Um… er… oh, of course: Mike! How lovely to hear from you!' If see a bit of yourself in that, work on it. You have the basic social instinct that makes a good salesperson, but are probably still a bit insecure. Relax; trust yourself and your natural sociability a bit more. Then people will start trusting you more.

Most social magnets are not butterflies. They are simply sociable, philanthropic (in its original sense of 'people-liking') individuals. And thus ideal material for specialist sales work, because in the end *people buy from people*: a motto that should be engraved above the door of every marketing department.

As I've said, I can spot a natural salesperson almost at once, and I'm very rarely wrong. It's like artistic or performing talent. Of course, talent is never enough: there must be training (not just an initial course, either, but regular updating – I advise sales people to go on a course every six months, to keep their skills sharp). But talent is the right, and the only, place to start.

people buy from people

There are, of course, other aspects to the sales personality – but I believe they are all secondary to being liked. This is my list:

Ambition. Like entrepreneurs, good salespeople are ambitious. Financially ambitious, but more: like entrepreneurs, they want to make a difference, to their company and to their customers. Ask them what they are most proud of, and it will probably be something they did to fix a big customer problem.

Persistent. Another trait salespeople share with entrepreneurs is not taking no for an answer. They often have to be more diplomatic about this than entrepreneurs, but the underlying determination is the same. Perhaps this should be expressed as not taking no for a *final* answer. Going away empty-handed from a meeting, the good salesperson either understands that the client was totally inappropriate, or mutters, 'I'll get the business next time, just watch me…'

Resilient. Good salespeople don't take rejection personally. See page 68 for more on this important aspect of the sales craft.

Intelligent. This is often overlooked, but very important. Salespeople need to know their markets, research customers and, above all, work out what customers really need, even when those customers are not being explicit. Sales is not a job for the dim-witted.

A listener. This is often the biggest weakness in an otherwise talented, natural salesperson. Which is disappointing, as listening is a skill that can easily be learnt once the individual understands the need to learn it. See page 50 for more on this.

Trustworthiness. This is an essential part of being a good salesperson. Proper sales should *never* go hand-in-hand with dishonesty. Many people assume that salespeople will be untrustworthy: if you can prove you are the opposite, your customers will like you. If you cannot, and are too much of a butterfly, you will lose them.

Empathy. There are all sorts of techniques for establishing empathy – mirroring body posture, phrasing things the client's way (and so on). While these are useful, especially in difficult situations, they are tricks, and will add falseness to your presentation if overused or used self-consciously. The natural salesperson is genuinely interested in people and gets to 'feel things their way' (up to a point, anyway) without resorting to tricks. Note that it is still well worthwhile learning to read body language. You need to pick up all the signals you can from the client.

Product knowledge is often cited as essential for a salesperson. Its absence is certainly bad news, but there is a danger in over-rating its importance and thinking that technical people can sell just because they know a lot about the product. They can't – unless they are also natural salespeople. A moderately well-informed person who is liked by the client is much more likely to sell than an expert about whom the client feels nothing in particular.

With technicians trying to be salespeople there is an ever-present risk of going on about features too much. The liked, non-expert sales natural can (and must) always admit it if they cannot answer a technical question, adding that they can find the answer out from an expert back at base – which they then, of course, must do.

What the liked non-expert must understand is customer pain. The salesperson needs to convince the buyer that their product will solve this pain. This is much better done by citing other happy customers than by describing the technology in great detail.

Market knowledge is more important than expert product knowledge: understanding the main drivers, competitors and customers (three Cs, for people who like snappy formulae: changes, competition, customers) and where your offer fits in. An intelligent salesperson will always be developing and refining this.

Note that for the radical new product, the market may still be unclear. Start-up sales cornerstones should not feel hampered by a lack of market knowledge: nobody else has it either. If the product takes off, they will soon become the experts.

Sales: the stereotype

None of the business students I described in the introduction said so, but I suspect this thought was at the back of their minds: salespeople suck. They're insincere, manipulative and dishonest. Think timeshare and used cars, or look at the examples in literature: *Elmer Gantry*, Willy Loman, those desperate, dodgy (and brilliantly acted) characters in *Glengarry Glen Ross*.

And, of course, there is some truth in this. But only some. The 'hard sell' is one tiny facet of what ▶▶

salespeople do, a small but sadly excessively visible one. If this weren't a Beermat book, there would probably now be a diagram called 'The Sales Perception Iceberg', showing a triangle with a wiggly line about nine tenths of the way up it, and 'hard selling' above the line and 'real selling' below.

Even 'hard selling' isn't all bad. A short spell of it, *as long as it is honest*, is good training. I began to learn the craft trying to sell an undifferentiated product (scaffolding) during a recession (the early 1980s), and I'm proud of the fact.

Another stereotype about selling is that it is a simple set of skills. The students who wanted to be strategists assumed they could get people in to sell their stuff, just as they could get someone in to fix a broken window if needed.

There is much more to Beermat selling than the mechanical performance of certain skills. The selling I will be talking about is strategic, demanding and challenging. It's about empathy, understanding customer needs and working to create real solutions to those needs. It's about forging and maintaining mutually beneficial, long-term relationships with customers. It lies at the heart of building businesses.

So step forward, salespeople, and take a bow! You are honourable and you are indispensable.

🍺Beermat.biz

The above, 'listed' sales virtues can be worked on and developed. Resilience can be a difficult one for some people. Intelligence is often seen as a given, but can be developed and assisted by hard work and focus. But there is something instinctive about the natural social magnet that cannot be learned. It's either in the genes – our ancestors needed such people to keep the tribe together – or it's learned and fixed at a very young age.

If you see yourself in this mirror, congratulations! You have the basic material to be a great specialist salesperson. In this book you will find what you need to turn your potential into real skill and success.

If you do not see yourself in the mirror, *don't worry*. There are still key roles you can, and must, play in the sales process. More on these later, too.

Finding good sales people

Start-ups often have difficulties in finding sales cornerstones. This is because they look for the wrong kind of person – or look at the salaries (and greed) of top salespeople, and despair. Actually they don't need 'big-hitters', but people who have the traits listed above, especially the magic one of being liked.

Start by looking at the salespeople in your network to see who fits the bill. Talk to them, see if they like you and your idea and if they fancy a gamble on your business. Remember that start-up cornerstones do not need to be full-time from Day One: the business can't afford to pay them. But make it clear that if the business flies, the job – and the twenty per cent cornerstone's stake – is theirs. Many natural salespeople have an adventurous streak and this will appeal to them.

If there is nobody in your network who fits this bill but you have contacts in the industry you are planning to sell to, talk to them. Whom, among the salespeople who come to them (especially who come selling undifferentiated things like photocopiers), do they really like? Can they put you in touch with this person? The individual in question might be ambitious and eager to sell something more interesting.

Failing that, find a 'social magnet' with no sales skills, and get them interested. Yes, they will have to learn selling, but they have many of the skills already. Send them on a course; give them this book; get them out there meeting people. Encourage them to find a sales mentor (see page 21). Coach them: they will make mistakes early on, but should learn fast if you talk through the mistakes in a way that does not attach blame but focuses on lesson-learning – the right way to motivate all your people.

If you have chosen the right kind of person and given them the right selling skills, you'll be amazed how quickly they become very good salesperson.

The same method applies to existing SMEs or partnerships in search of the right kind of salesperson to put fizz back into their sales efforts. They have an extra option not available to the start-up, of course, and that is to look round the existing members of the team to see who has the right personality. Try this first. You may already have a sales natural among you, in which case give them the job. Give them sales training, too, of course. That way you have someone with all the advantages of the insider – commitment, familiarity with (and membership of) the company culture, market knowledge – to add to their personality and the skills they will acquire.

If there is no such person, then follow the method recommended above for start-ups. Note that the 'find a salesperson who a) is bored by what they sell and b) you like' route will be easy: people will come selling to you already, so plenty of candidates should present themselves.

If none of these routes bear fruit, are you really serious about revamping your sales, or are you playing a game of 'yes, but' (see page 57)? There's always advertising and agencies, but these are a bit impersonal. You need someone who will be really committed to your organisation, not simply a 'gun for hire'.

And for cornerstones in search of entrepreneurs...

There is, of course, another side of the story. Supposing you are either an untrained sales natural, or a salesperson in search of a more interesting job than selling existing products for a large business…how do you set about finding a team to join?

The answer, naturally, dovetails with what we say above. Get networking. Join business networks. There are bound to be local ones, but I also recommend Thomas Power's international online network, Ecademy (www.ecademy.com). You're good at meeting people, so go out there and do it! More on this topic on page 46.

When deciding whether to commit to a business, trust your intuition about the individuals involved. Of course, they must make the right noises about having a serious business and about offering you a serious stake in that business if things go well. But do you trust them, both their competence and their honesty? Let the more cynical side of your usually good nature take over here: did you really like them? Really? Honestly?

If you're not sure, my advice is to move on. There are hundreds of start-ups out there who could use your special skills.

The metaphor of sexual relationships is entirely appropriate. Don't flirt and 'play hard to get': be very clear about what you need and want, and wait till it comes along.

Experienced salespeople may well face a drop in income if they move from a steady job to a start-up. Expect this: your reward is twofold. One: it is more exciting and interesting work; two: you get the chance to make really serious money. If you do make the change and the first venture fails, don't forget that being a sales cornerstone is an art in itself, which you will learn as you go along. I've done seventeen start-ups: some netted me excellent money, others were financial duds. Overall, I've done fine out of my life as a 'serial sales cornerstone', and have had intellectual and personal fulfilment – as well as lots of simple fun – on the way.

If you are up to your neck in mortgages, school fees etc then maybe a start-up is not for you. Try a more established business that has taken the messages of this book on board and wants to grow in the Beermat style...

The sales mentor

I advise entrepreneurs and intrapreneurs to find a mentor, but the same is true for sales people. Actually, I think it's true for anyone entering any profession which they intend to take seriously.

Remember that a mentor is someone who likes you and whom you like, and who has expertise in your area of study that they are eager to pass on. Most sales people go through bad patches, usually due to simple bad luck, but sometimes due to a loss of confidence. Talking things through with a mentor can help you across these wilderness times. In better times, you can swap stories and get endless small pieces of advice that never seem to get into books.

Finding specific sales mentors is harder than finding a general business mentor. For many salespeople it is a boss they worked for. I was lucky: my dad was a wonderful mentor. The best advice I can give is to be on the lookout for such a person, and to value them if you find them. As with all mentors (see the section on customer mentors later), make it rewarding for them, not financially but personally.

Sales styles

Although there is a distinct and specific sales personality, there are many ways in which that personality can express itself. It's like music, where many people share the quality of 'being musical' but all develop their own style.

That's why I dislike the use of standardised scripts for professional salespeople. Scripts, as you will see later, are brilliant props for non-salespeople forced into sales situations. For the true sales professional, they are an insult and a burden, like – keeping the music analogy going – asking a jazzer to play the same notes every evening. You've moved beyond that: develop your own selling style and use it with pride.

The drawback is that some customers won't like your style. Accept this fact. I've spoken to audiences, got rave reviews from almost everybody in the room and had one person who said my presentation was truly dreadful. You can't please everybody, and shouldn't try to: that way lies blandness and mediocrity. The same goes for selling. You can't sell to everybody. Don't expect to.

Be yourself, and concentrate your efforts on selling to people who respond favourably to that. At the same time, never stop improving your skills.

Chapter Three: The Key Sales Roles

Although I believe that people either have or don't have sales instincts – simple as that – the actual process of selling is complex. This is why non-salespeople can and should have a role in it. The sales natural is only part of the sales effort.

This is often not understood by people who think that sales is something that goes on in sales departments and which the rest of the business can ignore. Back to Stevenson's Law!

Everybody has to sell

It helps to break down the sales process into various roles (later in the book, I shall break it down another way, as it unfolds over time, but in keeping with my conviction that business is about people, I'll produce the cast list first and tell the story later).

The key roles are:

★ The telemarketer

★ The seeker after new business ('hunter')

★ The account manager ('farmer')

★ The sales manager

★ The information seeker

★ The evangelist

★ The customer mentor

★ Other external friends of the business

non-sales people **can** and **should** have a role

The sales team

Four of the above roles are played by what are usually regarded as salespeople. These are:

★ The telemarketer

★ The seeker after new business

★ The account manager

★ The sales manager

The *telemarketer* gets the whole process moving, garnering lists of prospects and providing initial qualification of those lists.

You do not have to be a sales natural to be a telemarketer, but it helps hugely. The natural's ease of manner and amiability gets people at the other end of the line talking, producing real, useful information rather than simple data. I shall explain why this matters, and say more on what telemarketers do and how to do it most effectively, in the section on page 84.

Please don't confuse this information-gathering role with tele*sales* – those people who phone you up at inconvenient times to 'have a chat about kitchens'. I dislike this method of selling, intensely. Beermat companies seeking to build good customer relations should avoid it.

The second category is *new business*. This is the most important sales role for most businesses. Get this right and you have a real chance of success; mess it up and you will be struggling. Much of this book is aimed at this kind of salesperson as a result.

The new business salesperson is sometimes referred to as a 'hunter'. He or she is out there, knocking on doors, meeting new people, finding out about their needs and what the company can do to meet these needs; always closing, closing, closing towards the deal.

The hunter has to be a sales natural. No exceptions.

The third category is *account management*. Once the deal has been done, a new kind of relationship is established with the customer, one which needs to be maintained. The hunter is not the best person to do this: a manager is required, who will build a long-term relationship with the client. Pure hunters lack the patience to do this.

Account managers are often referred to as farmers. They are usually sales naturals, but do not have to be: technical people who have a nice manner can become excellent farmers. Like hunters, their single most valuable trait is to be liked, but farmers are liked in a quieter way than the outgoing, charismatic hunter. They are, after all, building a long-term relationship. I imagine that the hunters are people you want to invite to a large party to make it go with a swing, while the farmer is more the ideal dinner-party guest, talking to everyone, keeping conversation bubbling, eventually perhaps getting into a long discussion with one other person on a subject on which that other person is an expert.

Hunter	Farmer
Must be liked	Must be liked
Enjoys risk	Risk-averse
Spontaneous	A planner
Impatient	Meticulous
Bored by company politics	Intrigued by company politics
Inspirational	Gets job done
Emotional	Logical
'Works' a room at a big gathering	Delightful guest at dinner party
Rock star	Record producer
Ideal material for sales cornerstone in start-up	Taken on once big accounts have been initiated by hunter

Beermat.biz

The 'forecourt' stereotype of salesperson is, of course, the hunter at his (or sometimes her) worst: pushy, deceitful, uncaring. The Beermat business, striving for repeat business and an excellent reputation, does not want such people representing it.

The worst type of farmer is the one who 'goes native' and starts acting as if they were a rather bureaucratically-minded employee of the companies whose accounts they are supposed to be managing on their employer's behalf.

Note that in a start-up or very small business, you cannot afford both. The start-up sales cornerstone must be a hunter, who will have to learn a few basic farming skills. As the business grows, the sales cornerstone will need to hire subordinates: farmers if they can build large, long-term accounts with big customers; a mixture of hunters and farmers if the average transaction size is small and growth will come from lots and lots of new business.

Another term for the two roles is 'killers' and 'cookers'. But I don't feel this captures the Beermat spirit of working with clients to create long-term, mutually beneficial relationships.

The final category of traditional salesperson is the *sales manager*. Good sales managers usually do their spell as salespeople out there – farming or hunting, depending on their character – then get promoted and thrive on the responsibility.

It's not everybody's cup of tea, however: some hunters hate it. I'm one – managers spend far too much time looking at spreadsheets and not enough time selling. This can be a problem in a sapling start-up: the sales cornerstone may feel like me, and become demotivated by what appear to others to be 'exciting new responsibilities'.

There are two aspects of sales management. One is keeping an eagle eye on sales figures. Non-salespeople can do this, often better than salespeople. The other is motivating the staff. Commissions and targets are the usual mechanisms. I hate commissions – see the box overleaf. Targets, on the other hand, are essential. But don't just use them as a threat. If a salesperson is underperforming, good sales managers will coach them, for example, by going with them on a sales visit and spotting what they are doing wrong – there is almost always something. If they continue to miss their targets, of course, they have to go. In a small company, if they are liked and are good team players, they might flourish elsewhere in the outfit. Give them the chance.

Commission? No, thanks

I am very against remunerating salespeople via commission, especially in small companies. It encourages salespeople to distance themselves from what the rest of the business does – a big mistake. If an SME wants to regain some of that start-up passion, it must recreate the culture of a start-up, which is tribal and collective. 'One for all, and all for one' is the motto. Such an attitude is not fostered by bloated sales commissions. Instead salespeople should be paid a decent salary, and a bonus based on the overall performance of the business, just like everyone else in the team.

Actually, I dislike sales commissions in any size of organisation. The current pensions 'mis-selling' – what a wonderful euphemism! – scandal was caused by commission-hungry salespeople more interested in quick bucks than the welfare of the client. I'm delighted to see that the firms that motivated their sales forces in this way are now facing large bills as a consequence.

Yes, a non-commission approach will scare off some salespeople. Fine: they are not the team players you need, anyway.

Beermat.biz

Note that in a very small partnership, SME or start-up, you may not be able to afford a sales manager. The sales cornerstone/hunter should report to the board members, who can use the Beermat Sales Pipeline, which I shall introduce later (see page 118) to make sure the sales team is pulling its weight.

I am horrified by the appalling quality of sales management I see in many start-ups and SMEs (and even in some big companies). The sales 'managers' are incredibly vague about the status of potential sales – are they likely to happen or not? Nobody seems to know. Sales staff receive little coaching.

There is a simple way of tracking the progress of sales: the Beermat Sales Pipeline. When I started teaching sales, I didn't really talk about this, assuming everybody had something similar; I might as well remind people to open the office door before trying to walk through it. Then one day I did describe the pipeline, and the client was so surprised and so grateful that I now put it at the heart of every sales talk I do. If you learn one thing from this book and that is the Beermat Sales Pipeline, then you've struck gold.

But there's plenty of ground to cover first…

Roles for the rest of the team

These are:

★ The information seeker

★ The evangelist

The sales team are your key 'eyes and ears' in the marketplace, but they need support from everybody else in the organisation. How is this support best provided?

The simplest way is by engaging individuals in conversation. Especially people's peers: technical types are particularly good at this, discussing with fellow experts the demerits of their various employers' systems or the latest developments in the technology over pints of ale.

Valuable business intelligence can often emerge from such conversations. If the employer of the person your techie is talking to is a potential customer, and the subject is a huge problem in your specialist area – 'You guys could sort it out, I'm sure, but we never seem to hear from you' – your business has just acquired a golden sales lead.

If this happens, the non-salesperson should resist any temptation they may feel to 'try their hand at a bit of hunting'. They should just get the business card of the person they are talking to, and next day pass the information on to the sales specialists, who will then pursue the lead.

What the non-specialist can do is a bit of gentle *farming*. Keep an eye on the process. A few days after passing the info to the sales department, call the contact to see if the salespeople have been in touch and if so, how they got on. The answer to the first question should be 'yes' and to the second 'well' – but this is not always the case. If the salespeople haven't been in touch, you are right to contact your salespeople and ask why not. Salespeople have no right to get stroppy at 'someone else telling us our job' under these circumstances. They should have made that call!

your business
has just **acquired** a golden
sales lead

If the call did not go well, the situation can still be saved. Not every salesperson suits every prospect: maybe the person who called was too pushy. Apologise on behalf of the firm, and ask if it's OK to have someone else less forceful make contact. Remember there should be no problem with this, as the prospect has a real problem you could solve. Then get back to the sales department, tell them what happened and ask for a more suitable salesperson to call. Once again, you are right to do this, and if they start whining about being told their job – tell them you read it here and blame it on me!

Of course, it may be that the contact is a time-waster, in which case the salespeople should tell you that, and you should accept what they say.

If you are the *boss*, how can you ensure that your people do as much information-gathering as they can?

Firstly, make sure they understand how to network. This key twenty-first century business skill is becoming easier and easier to do, as the dos and don'ts become better understood, as formal networking forums develop, as the notion loses the stigma it once had and becomes regarded as good, sociable behaviour. For more on this important topic, see the chapter on the Craft of Selling.

Secondly, you should reward non-salespeople who network well. A good starter is to allow everyone in the business to get some expenses for networking. If someone, even the post boy, produces a batch of business cards after an evening at the pub, they should get the price of a couple of rounds. If these generate leads, some form of bonus is in order. Clearly, the 'money for cards' system needs a level of trust to make it work – you don't want people wandering into pubs offering drinks all round for an indiscriminate collection of business cards. So explain to everyone the purpose of the system (e.g. by giving them this book to read) and tell them you are trusting them.

Your people also need to be *evangelists* for your product. The word can summon up images of ranting hot-gospellers on American TV (who usually turn out to have mistresses, underworld connections etc). I mean something a bit different: your people should know about your products and why they are the best for certain types of pain, and be prepared to talk about them to interested outsiders. The original gospel was probably spread as much by quiet conversation as by hellfire preaching – though the Reverend Arthur E. Southon was, apparently, expert at both types of 'sell'!

Are you all evangelists?

★ What is the elevator pitch of your business (remember 'exactly what it is you do, for whom, and why should they buy it from you')?

★ Does everyone in your business know it?

★ Can they recite it, here, now?

★ Can they get its message across informally, if asked in a pub 'what does the company do?' (and not sound like a bad PR spokesperson)?

★ Can *you* recite it, here, now?

★ Can *you* get its message across informally, if asked in a pub 'what does the company do?' (and not sound like a bad PR spokesperson)?

★ What is your best client story – not the funniest, but the one where you have delivered most value?

▶▶

★ Does everyone in your business know it?

★ Do they understand it; do they really see what a great thing it was you did for the client?

★ Do you understand it; do you really see what a great thing it was you did for the client?

★ When your people talk about working for you, what do they talk about? What a mean sod you are or what a great character you are? What a pain it is or what fun it is?

★ Do all your people have business cards, even the drivers and machinists? Do they understand the rules and skills of networking? Are they rewarded for getting sales leads?

Beermat.biz

Outsiders

I've already mentioned the value of personal mentors. The *customer mentor* is a refinement of this idea. As with a personal mentor, a customer mentor is a customer who likes you, whom you like and who understands the value in what you offer.

Customer mentors help you design the product in the first place, by being honest and trusting about what they really need from it. They will act as evangelists for you within their organisation. They can give you general market information and, if they are older and more experienced, general business advice. They may suggest sales leads, or, better still, actually provide referrals, either one-to-one by saying 'mention my name when you speak to Bill' or by allowing you to cite them as a general endorser, both of which can be hugely helpful.

How do you get such a mentor? There is no formula. The person just has to like you, and value what you do. And then you have to ask for the above favours.

Why should they help you out? Partially because it is in their interest to do so. They will get prestige within their organisation for introducing you and your fantastic product. They want you to do well, as they value what you do and don't want you going bust. They don't want the hassle of sourcing something similar from someone else. But at the end of the day, people become customer mentors because they like you.

Make it fun for them. Listen to them. Act on any advice they give you and let them know how you got on. Get them involved in projects. 'What can we do next?' is what you want to hear from your customer mentor. Remember they are doing this because they like it, not because they have to.

The best of these becomes, of course, a real friend. They always say that you shouldn't mix the personal with business. I disagree. Business is about people. There are, of course, boundaries, similar to those in public life generally. Avoid sexual entanglements. Know how far you can confide in someone – like any friendship, intimacy usually takes time to develop. Be open about 'wearing hats' (as in the line 'As a friend, I say x; but wearing my business hat, I have to say y…')

The ideal customer mentor is also a bit of a maven (see page 131). They love gathering and disseminating information about the industry where they work: they will be interested in you because you have something new to offer or you are a new (and likeable) face on the 'scene'.

Customer mentors on a Beermat

★ A customer…

★ Who likes you…

★ And whom you like…

★ And who understands the value in your product

He or she will:

★ Work with you on a new project

★ Co-write the White Paper

★ Network you within their organisation

★ Suggest sales leads

★ Provide one-to-one referrals

★ Act as general endorser (e.g. for Beermat intro email: see page 90)

Beermat.biz

Note that, as with close friends, there is a limit to the number of mentors one can have. But that limit is not one! In practice, good salespeople have a few close customer mentors, plus a number of 'customer pals' who will help out to a lesser degree than the mentor.

For example, many customers, if truly delighted with your work, will be happy to make a few referrals. These are very valuable: make sure you always ask happy customers if they are prepared to do this, or to provide an endorsement.

Other outsiders can help the business, too, though none are as valuable as the customer mentor. I shall discuss them in a later section on 'connectors, mavens and persuaders' (see page 131). For the moment, just note that such people are available and will help you if you have a good product (and if you motivate them to do so).

So there are the key sales roles. Four are formal sales roles (though only one of them absolutely has to be performed by 'natural' salespeople); two are for everyone else within the business; two are key outsiders. *All* these roles need to be filled to ensure a dynamic sales process that not only creates a pipeline of sales leads, but makes sure that the business is listening closely to the market and its ever-changing requirements.

The sales cornerstone

There is one role I didn't cover specifically cover above, though it gets a number of mentions. That is the sales cornerstone. This role is specific to start-ups.

The cornerstone, as I've said, needs to be a hunter, as their prime job is to get business. They also play a key role in the development of the product – a topic I discuss in chapter six. In a Beermat start-up they are a joint owner of the company, and thus need to be able to discuss strategy. They also need to be robust enough to stand up to entrepreneurs, who are usually forceful characters (to put it politely!). Personally, I can't think of a more exciting job.

An SME with an existing ownership structure, but which wants to build revenue fast, should consider creating more equity to motivate a sales cornerstone figure. If this is impossible, pay large bonuses based on the overall performance of the business.

Sales Functions on a Beermat

★ Pure telemarketers

- Produce a list of prospects…
- …with information (= early qualification)
- Sales personality helps

★ Hunters

- Open doors
- 'Always Closing'
- Right person to be sales cornerstone in start-up
- Strictly for 'natural' salespeople only

★ Farmers

- Account management
- Sales personality helps, but pleasant technical people can master art

★ Sales Managers

- In charge of the whole process
- Need Beermat Sales Pipeline
- A managerial job: should understand sales process, but do not need sales personality

▶▶

★ **Information gatherers**

- Everyone else in the team

- Use networking skills and opportunities

★ **Evangelists**

★ **Customer mentors**

- Hugely valuable allies

- More than one possible. Also have 'customer pals'

★ **Other external friends of the business**

- 'Connectors, mavens and persuaders' – see page 131

★ **The Sales Cornerstone**

- Performs all the 'sales specialist' roles in a start-up

⬤Beermat.biz

Chapter Four: # The Elements of Selling: Qualifying and Closing

These are the two most important elements of selling in any and every business.

Qualifying is about finding prospects, and, more important, finding out about them, so you understand their overall situation, specific needs and, very important, ability to pay.

Closing is actually getting people to make a commitment, such as (but not just) signing on the dotted line.

When giving my 'Sales on a Beermat' presentation, I always ask the audience which of these two activities they consider the most difficult. I usually get a pretty even split of answers. I then ask them why they answered as they did.

Qualifying is hardest, say one group, because it takes more time and effort. You might have to start from a position of total ignorance, then slowly compile a list of prospects, then find out details of these companies – size, specialism etc – then get names of people within them, then get the names of the *right* people within them... This is time-consuming and tiring.

Yes, the others reply, but there's little real stress involved. You just have to be methodical, persistent and sometimes use a little imagination. Closing, however, involves psychology, putting pressure on people, and thus – as my audiences are not made up of sadists – putting pressure on yourself. It may even involve asking for money, something all of us, even the natural salespeople, find hard to do.

Which of the two sections of the audience is right? Or is there no right and wrong, just 'different strokes for different folks'?

I say closing is the easiest. Why? Because if the qualification has been done properly, closing should be easy. Closing only becomes hell if the customer has not been properly qualified. Poorly qualified customers:

★ don't really want the product at all, *or*

★ do want the product but are already sourcing it from another supplier, with whom they are happy (not a total disaster, but certainly an extra hurdle), *or*

★ have no budget, *or*

★ the company has a budget but the person you have been talking to lacks the power to deploy it, *or*

★ it's a large contract with a seemingly endless series of hoops to jump through – fine for a large business, but a potential disaster for the small organisation (more on this later)

However, to qualify well, you have to do some closing. In truth, we have to move beyond the traditional distinction between qualifying and closing. This distinction creates the myth that sales is a lot of research plus a one-off visit where you ask for money. This is rarely the case, however much the day-to-day sales practice of a big consumer-goods company may seem that way. In reality, qualifying and closing merge seamlessly. Good salespeople begin making small closes as soon as they engage with a customer, not to get money, but to build trust and to get information – in other words, to advance the qualification process.

Yes, at the very start of the 'sales story', when you are trawling directories for names to put on a list, you are doing pure qualification. And at the end of the story (the hunter's story, anyway), when you ask for the customer's signature, you have pure closing. But those are the only times when you are just doing one or the other. The rest of the sales process is a mixture of both.

This is the real meaning of the oft-quoted motto ABC – Always Be Closing. It doesn't mean 'ask for the business straight off', but 'Qualify Relentlessly Through A Series Of Small Closes, Until The Final, Pure Close'. But QRTASOSCUTFPC, although the name of an obscure Aztec god, isn't so catchy an acronym, so I tell people to remember ABC.

always be closing

An example of ABC in action… You've been given the name of a potential client, and contact them asking for a meeting. This is an attempt at a close. You are asking for a commitment from them. Yes, it's only fifteen minutes of their time, but that time could be valuable. They say yes. A small close, a small sign that they are at least in theory interested in your product. You fix a time and a place. They're being specific: another small close.

But at the same time, this has also been qualification. You now have reason to believe that the person you had on your list is a) still with the company, b) probably around the right level to be dealing with, and c) has a vague interest.

In that first, fifteen-minute meeting, you are practising your listening skills and finding out about both the company and the individual. Pure qualification? Possibly, so make sure that you end the meeting with some kind of close – an agreement to a longer meeting, maybe with someone else closer to the key issue that has emerged in your discussion.

At this next meeting, you must do a lot of listening and learning (still more qualification) but you will be seeking further commitment from the customer, too. Ideally this should take the form of a sanity check (see page 103).

Finally, you will reach that moment of 'pure closure', when you know exactly what the client needs, exactly what they can afford, exactly what you can do to help them meet their needs, exactly how much they are going to pay for it, and that they want *you* do the work or deliver the product rather than one of your rivals. It's time for the person whom you know to be the right individual to sign the contract.

The final close

Hunters live for closing – but it can still be a difficult moment.

Even experienced hunters often have trouble *asking for money*. But as a salesperson you have to overcome this. If the client is eager to buy, it is your job to sell them what you offer, at the best possible sustainable price ('sustainable' is very important:

we're talking long-term relationships here). You must discipline yourself to ask for business and ask for the right price for that business.

If it's tough for the battle-hardened hunter, what about the non-salesperson forced by circumstance into a selling role? Especially if they run their own business, and are effectively asking for money for themselves?

The solution, both for the non-specialist and the hunter suddenly affected by a loss of self-belief, is to write a script, as short as possible. Then learn it, practice it and use it, parrot-fashion, at the moment of closing. I dislike sales scripts and the bored, insincere voices that always go with them, but this is the one (and only) time when they come into their own.

'Excellent. The widgets are £50 plus VAT. How many would you like?'

Say it. On autopilot – just let the words come out.

Then keep quiet and wait for the answer to the 'open' question you asked. If you get the right one, proceed with the next line in the script.

'So you want one hundred widgets. At £50 each, plus VAT, that's (takes out calculator and works out sum) *£5,875.* (Smiles and produces order form.) *If you'd just to sign here, then I'll get the order processed straight away and they'll be with you in two weeks.'*

Then fall silent again.

My dad, who was a superb salesman, taught me the value of silence. The moment the prospect has agreed that your product fulfils their need, that they can afford it and have a current budget for it, and – hurrah! – they are going to buy it; and you have given them the order form, and (if necessary) given them a pen to sign it with…

Shut up.

Silence.

The moments that follow can be the longest of your life. Do not say anything. Do not send any body signals. Don't make eye contact. Don't do anything that 'breaks the state', or even offers the chance to amend that state a little.

They should sign. Supposing they start backtracking instead?

Make confident eye contact. Sit straight and proud, maybe leaning forward a little. Systematically run over all the points of agreement you have already established (otherwise they would not have been just about to sign). Remind them of the benefits of what you have to offer. If they come up with objections, meet them. Stay cool, stay patient – but do not budge. Think attrition. It took the Allies four years to break the German lines in the First World War. You can sit in this office for another hour…

When you have done the deal, smile, shake hands and leave. I've seen salespeople, overcome with the joy and matiness of having just signed a deal, try to start selling something else. Don't. This kills the atmosphere, which should be one of contented closure and optimism about the next phase. Come back later.

Closing on a Beermat

Script

Silence

That's it!

⬛ Beermat.biz

The above section may seem harsh to some readers (non-salespeople, especially), so remember that the Beermat businesses provide real solutions for long-term customers at fair prices. So you are creating a win–win situation here, not trying to 'get one over' on the guy opposite. That person is sweating and prevaricating now because that is a natural reaction to the inevitable stress attendant on decision-making, *not* because you're about to con him or her. Their reason and self-interest will prevail if you let them.

If you *are* trying to con someone – please don't. You're giving sales, which is a respectable and essential profession, a bad name.

Chapter Five: The Craft of Selling

Qualifying and closing are the key elements of selling, but there are many other aspects of the craft. As with salesperson traits, different writers will produce different lists. Here's mine:

★ Networking

★ Listening

★ Meetings

★ Avoiding 'games'

★ Negotiating

★ Buying signals

★ Objections

★ Dealing with rejection

★ Time management

Dealing with them in order…

The art of networking

Networking is a key aspect of modern sales, especially for start-ups, SMEs and partnerships. It is a fashionable topic at the moment, but it is actually what all sales naturals – and able business people generally – have always done. Masons have networked since time immemorial; the City of London's guildhalls were networking centres in the Middle Ages; in 1776 Adam Smith complained about merchants' propensity to network and form cabals.

What has changed recently is the rise of semi-formal networks, driven by the Internet. I say semi-formal because they have rules but entry is a lot easier than old-fashioned clubs.

I run such a network myself – please pop along to a monthly 'Beermat Monday' session, details can be viewed on my website www.beermat.biz

Twenty-first century networking begins online. Find a networking group you like the look of and get involved, posting a profile of yourself and participating in discussion groups. Once you have a number of e-acquaintances, find out when there is a live event: all good networks will have an offline, live component. Check who is attending the event (the good online networks will provide this information), and don't forget to sign up formally yourself. Prepare a list of people you want to meet, and a 'conversation opener' for each one, based on something you have in common (remember, the network will provide lists of attendees at events, and, elsewhere on the system, they will have left profiles of themselves). Don't feel this is 'artificial'. It is, of course, but it is only a way of getting over initial hurdles: the real stuff of personal chemistry will follow (or not) later.

At the event, don't panic and lose the courage to approach people. Remember, that's what the event is for. Think 'speed dating': you don't get any points for lurking in the corner. Use your opener, and talk for a couple of minutes. If it feels right, escalate the level of intimacy from a simple exchange of facts ('Where do you live?') to an exchange of feelings ('Do you like living in X?'). This is a good test of rapport: if this is forming, the person will venture a response with emotional content. If they don't venture such a response, and shut down instead (effectively saying 'none of your business'), then rapport is not building. Best back off and look elsewhere.

Don't forget that this is a two-way process – offer an emotion ('I love living in London') as well. Though this looks like a 'technique' (and is one; it comes from neuro-linguistic programming), it won't work if used mechanically. You need to be genuinely interested in what the other person has to say ('social magnets' are interested; they like people and want to hear what people have to say).

However the conversation goes, break it off after a few minutes and swap cards. If you liked the person, make it clear that you will be in touch.

you need to be genuinely **interested** in what the other person has to **say**

Note that in the old days it might have been rude to keep conversations brief, but this is not the case when networking. The cardinal sin at an event like this is to monopolise people.

As with all meetings, go through the business cards you collected the next day and make a note on each person – did you like them; if so, what were their interests? Then follow up (back online again) the leads you want to. A simple 'nice to meet you at the Z event the other day…' email is a good start.

Over time, you will build your own network of people you have met and liked at these events. Turn yourself into a 'network node': the centre of a network. This network is of huge value to you, so keep it alive. Nudge members regularly with appropriate material – 'Did you hear about X?' 'Here's something interesting I read the other day...'

This network can become huge, as you don't have to remember everyone – keep their details easily accessible on your computer. In practice, network members will fall into categories:

★ The few you speak to regularly

★ People you would recognise in the street, out of context

★ People you remember when they call up

★ People you need a 'jog' to recall

Note that this isn't a simple hierarchy of likeability. Even people in the latter category are there because you liked them: if you suddenly start doing business with them, they can move up to the top category instantly.

Stage your network's own real 'live' events. That's what people who give lots of parties have always done. I hold 'Beermat Monday' events once a month, when people can come and meet me in a pub – though they spend much more time talking to one another.

Sole traders, by which I mean all one-person businesses (including many franchisees), not just people who call themselves 'sole traders' for tax purposes, have to network like crazy. Not just with peers, either: you must play the full sales role and get out there and network with potential customers. This is not easy for people who are not natural self-promoters, but there's nobody else to do it, so you just have to summon up the courage and go for it.

Remember the rules. You are not here to sell, sell, sell; just to establish contacts. Talk about your work; tell people why it's interesting and what you love about it (most people relate to enthusiasm and interest). If you can work a few comments about customer benefits into the story, great. At the same time, ask about the other person's work and any issues they have. Remember that Magic Question: 'Where's the pain?' If you really think you can help them, ask if you can call to arrange a meeting, get a business card, then call during work hours.

Listening

Of all the sales attributes, 'being a good listener' is the one that is most easily learned. Follow the points below, and you will find your sales skill increasing with great speed. You will probably get more enjoyment from selling, too: relax, you're not there to make a big song and dance, but to find out about customer pain and then talk through what can be done about it.

Let the other person lead the conversation. Ordinary social conversation tends to be a bit like tennis, with the initiative going from person to person then back again. One person may say they went to Beijing last year, then another may then chime in with 'I've been there as well'. In doing so, the 'chimer-in' leads the conversation away from the first person's experiences to their own. This is sometimes done in a competitive spirit – 'Oh, yes, Beijing. Very overrated. Have you been to Ulaanbataar?' – but more often it is just a natural instinct to convey information.

A good listener fights back their instinct to 'chime in', and keeps their focus permanently on the *customer's* story and views.

Spot 'hot buttons'. Customers will emphasise certain words or phrases in their speech, which is a sure sign that they feel particularly strongly about them. Note these, and form a question about them or ask them to elaborate: 'Tell me more about that…' This is not 'chiming in', as it keeps the conversational ball firmly in the other person's court. 'Buying signals' are the salesperson's favourite hot button – more on these later.

Ask open questions. Make sure your questions invite the other person to say more, as opposed to *closed* questions, which just aim for a yes or no answer. Open questions are introduced with interrogatives like 'How…?' 'When…?' etc. Rudyard Kipling, who was a professional journalist before becoming a novelist and poet, understood their value. His ever-curious 'elephant's child' says:

> *I keep six honest serving-men,*
> *They taught me all I knew;*
> *Their names are What and Where and When*
> *And How and Why and Who.*

Note that of these serving-men, 'why?' needs to be used with the most caution: it can be taken as confrontational. 'Why' is probably best prefaced by a compliment, e.g. 'That's interesting – why do you say that?'

Stay authentic. Early in Chris's career, someone told him that salespeople must always agree with the person they are talking to, to create empathy. This isn't always easy. If someone expresses a view you find unattractive, it will be false to express agreement, and this will show up. So don't. At the same time, don't get into an argument. Often the comment can simply be ignored. If pressed, agree that the topic is a difficult one – 'but let's get back to business'. If you are sincere about wanting to uncover your client's needs and (the key bit) about helping him or her solve them, this last response won't come across as phoney – because it won't be.

In fact you are less likely to do business with this person than with someone with whom your views are in some kind of harmony. I don't mean precise political allegiances, but more general attitudes to life. Remember my comments on 'sales style' and accept this.

Remember what you're there for. A key to listening well is to keep reminding yourself why you are there – to find out what the customer's issues are, and how you can help him or her.

Getting the best from meetings

The effective conduct of *meetings* is another important sales skill – well, it's a business skill that everyone should master, but it is particularly important for salespeople (or non-salespeople forced into a sales role). In the next chapter, I shall talk in detail about a special kind of meeting: the initial, fifteen-minute meeting between salesperson and prospect. The material here is of a more general nature. Seasoned meeting-goers may find it all obvious, but I've been going to meetings for twenty-five years and still get stuff wrong, so it's worth a read (or maybe it's me…).

Look smart and appropriate. Entering a new area of business, you may not know what is 'standard wear'. Turning up at a record company in a pinstripe suit, or at a City bank in jeans, will strike the wrong note. If in doubt, wear a suit – you can always pull off the tie and make yourself look casual, but it's hard to go the other way. Other aspects of self-presentation (cleanliness, tidiness etc) should be obvious, but it's always worth remembering this as it's stupid to lose business by doing it wrong.

Bring:

★ **Writing implements** and **paper**.

★ Plenty of **business cards** in good condition. I once attended a meeting where I was handed a tatty piece of paper with the bloke's name on, accompanied by a comment to the effect that he thought business cards were unnecessary. Everyone else, who had produced proper cards, felt a little embarrassed, and things went downhill from there.

★ A list of **questions** you want to ask. You can reread it while sitting in reception. In the meeting, just have it in front of you. Don't follow it mechanically, unless driven to do so by silence. Let conversation follow its natural course, tick off topics as they occur, then bring up any undiscussed issues at the end.

★ Your **brain**.

Leave plenty of **time** before you set off. It's rude – and unprofessional – to be late. Also, ten minutes sitting in reception watching the comings and goings can be instructive. (Don't be overawed by receptions. They are there to impress, like the fake bonhomie of the worst kind of salesperson. Remember this is a façade. But it can still be an informative one.)

While you're waiting there, **talk to the receptionist**. The natural salesperson will strike up a rapport with this person, and he or she can become a huge ally.

When the prospect appears, **smile, shake hands and make eye contact** with them. Remember this isn't an interrogation but the start of a potential mutually beneficial relationship.

When you sit down, **give your card** to everyone present (not just to people who look important). When they give their cards back to you, arrange them around you so that the card is along your line of sight to that person. So if you forget their name, just glance down…

Use everyone's **name** early in the conversation. People like the sound of their own name, and it will also lodge the name in your mind (an old Dale Carnegie trick: it did well enough for him!).

A few **pleasantries** to get things going are fine. But don't feel embarrassed to say after a minute or so: 'But let's get down to business!' A simple gesture like straightening papers, picking up a pen or putting a briefcase on to the floor may be enough to 'break the state' and set the new, businesslike tone.

Don't **hand out brochures**, factsheets (or any documents) mid-meeting, as this always distracts people. (It's easy to hide behind brochures. Your voice, personality and intelligence are better selling tools than any amount of paper.) Similarly, if given reading matter early on, take a brief look, then say something like, 'I'll read this properly later, if I may…' and put it to one side.

Do take **notes**. Don't be afraid to ask for a break in conversation to write something down (unless you do it too often), or to ask for someone to repeat something if you were busy noting when they spoke. These notes will be valuable later.

Keep making **eye contact** with people. This is a kind of social skill that comes naturally to good salespeople: it's a balancing act, between staring at someone (unnerving) and perpetually avoiding their gaze (even more unnerving).

Remember to work towards your goal. You are there to establish common ground – their needs, your capacity to meet them – and to emerge with some clearly defined, agreed **outcome**.

If you feel conversation is wandering off in an irrelevant direction, you have every right to say, 'but let's get back to these widget costs…' If you feel **conversation is wandering** off in an unexpected but interesting direction, go with it. If the other person then tries to rein it in, consider arranging to meet to talk about the new topic another time.

If you have asked for a chunk of someone's time, make sure you **don't overrun**. Fifteen minutes means fifteen minutes. For other meetings – can you get the stuff done in an hour?

In long meetings, a comfort break ten minutes before the end allows both parties time to step out of the meeting and reflect.

If you are getting on well, ask to be shown round the premises. Prospects like doing this, and it cements the relationship. Similarly, ask for brochures, stuff about the company (and so on). These rarely contain useful information, but the acceptance of them has a **ritual** quality that transcends their factual value.

Make sure you leave the meeting with **clear agendas** all round. What do you need to do next? What has the prospect promised to do?

After the meeting, **read through your notes** and check they cover the ground. Do this soon, as memory can quickly fade.

Do everything on your **agenda list**. Nudge the prospect after a week or two: 'You said you'd do X…'.

Finally, an essential piece of meeting etiquette for salespeople is: 'Don't diss the opposition'. I covered this in *The Beermat Entrepreneur*, but it's so important that I'll restate it here. The subject of rivals will undoubtedly emerge in meetings, and novice salespeople (and some experienced ones) feel this is a chance to show why their product is better. Especially by telling those horror stories they've heard about the rivals' after-sales service, or product reliability, or the drink habit of the CEO, or…

Don't go there. It is undignified and unprofessional. It sets a negative tone on the proceedings, when you want to keep things positive. It moves conversation away from what really matters, the prospect's 'pain' and what you can do to solve it. It may also be an insult to the prospect: if they currently use your rival's products, are you telling them they're stupid? Clearly, if the prospect says they have been using ABC widgets for a while *and are dissatisfied*, this is a huge buying signal (see below) and must be followed up. But let them do the complaining. Your job is to make everything better again.

If somebody tries to elicit a 'slagging-off' game by *praising* your rivals, don't get involved. Instead, treat it as useful information. Exactly how good are they? What do you *really* have to do to beat them? When you have learned all you can, simply comment that you hope to beat that. If the service does sound brilliant, admit it − but add your determination to top it. If it actually doesn't sound much, just say that you intend to do better than that. Stick to this line if pressed for a judgement.

As with all lists of dos and don'ts, make these a habit, and you will find yourself enjoying meetings more and more. Don't turn into a meetings junkie, that's all…

Games

Transactional Analysis (TA) was a management psychology fad back in the Eighties. It went the way of all fads − not just obscurity, but becoming a positive embarrassment, like flared trousers or kipper ties. It did not deserve this: TA contained useful material, especially the notion of 'games'. The effective salesperson understands these, and avoids them wherever possible.

Games in TA are played subconsciously by insecure or bored people. They usually involve creating unnecessary drama out of situations, wheeling in big emotions when small ones will suffice. Game-players like to act out roles as Rescuers, Persecutors or Victims – and, to add to the fun, to switch roles mid-game. If they did this on their own, this would be a minor problem, but they also rope in unsuspecting bystanders. In order for them to play their roles, they have to cast someone else in a complimentary role – for example a bully (Persecutor) needs a Victim. But they then need to switch, often to a Victim when their bullying is exposed ('It's not my fault I'm so aggressive…').

If you feel that someone is acting one of these roles – you may feel yourself being nudged in the direction of a complimentary role (some Victim-y people are brilliant at bringing out the worst in everybody else) – watch out. A big role-switch may be on its way. Suddenly, and you're not really sure how it happened, you're the Victim.

A classic game is called 'Yes, but…' Someone talks about a problem. You offer a solution. They reply, 'Yes, but…' You accept the objection, and offer another solution. The same reply. You offer a third solution. 'Yes, but…' The climax of this game is that the problem-ridden individual suddenly turns on you with a comment along the lines of , 'You're no help!'

This kind of pathological 'yes, but' mustn't be confused with genuine objections. Most objections are perfectly reasonable: it's only when you encounter a stream of them, especially when accompanied by an increasingly whiny tone, that you can reckon the 'Yes, but…' game is going on.

Sir Clive Woodward calls habitual TA game-players 'energy-sappers', and after a few encounters with them you will know why. People like this need therapy, and it's not your job to provide it (unless, of course, you are a therapist: a fine one-person business). They are best avoided, as they will play all sorts of other games later, for example about payment. If you cannot avoid them, watch out for the games. Stick to facts, be very clear about everything (game-players thrive on uncertainty) and be prepared walk away if you feel yourself being driven completely up the wall.

Of course, games played *consciously* can be fun and create rapport. Banter, for example. When I went to sell a new training product to a former employee who had gone on to great things, his first words to me were, 'Whatever you're selling, Mike, I don't want it!' But this was said with a smile, and in a tone that made it perfectly clear this was a joke, and we went on to do excellent, mutually beneficial business. It's the subconscious games, born of deep unhappiness, that cause the trouble.

Negotiating

Endless amounts have been written on this topic. To save acres of rainforest I will keep my comments on this topic to two essentials: discounts and overpromising.

Don't offer *discounts*. Studies show that if you allow salespeople leeway to give discounts, they will not only end up conceding those discounts to get the deal, but actually sell less product. So have a no-discount policy. Non-professional purchasers ask for discounts because they feel they ought to, and don't really mind being told that this is a fair price. Purchasing directors will tell you they have to get a discount. Do they *have* to, or do they get a huge buzz from doing so?

Occasionally, a discount turns into a 'deal-breaker'. If this is really the case, you may have to concede, as long as the discount still leaves you with a sensible margin. Make sure you get something in return. Favourable payment terms, for example. Beermat businesses, funding from revenue, need payment up front wherever possible. Always stick out for at least fifty per cent up front.

And here's a mistake I have made many times, and have seen other people make even more often. Don't get carried away and offer too much. It's no good cutting a brilliant deal where you got the full price and full advance payment if you agreed to deliver eighty tons of stuff tomorrow and you have nothing in stock and it takes a week to make. Yes, *in the long term* you should always assume infinite capacity to deliver – because that is true: if a deal is that important, you can get a strategic ally to help you deliver if you have enough time. What turns ambitious promises into commercial suicide notes are time constraints.

The correct answer to the request for eighty tons is to say: '*Yes, of course we can deliver it, but let me get back to you about timing.*'

If there is any likelihood of your getting carried away and overpromising, learn the above line as a script.

Buying signals

These are much more fun! Be on the lookout for them from the moment you first contact the prospect. You may have just struck lucky – a supplier has let them down, they need what you've got right now. If they send these signals, for heaven's sake act on them. Don't wait for a formal courtship process to work itself through. Yes, of course courtship is usually necessary, but never discount the lucky break.

That is probably the most important thing to know about buying signals: how often salespeople overlook them. Reasons? Because they don't expect them; because they lack sympathy; worst of all, because they have a standard sales routine that they aren't going to let anything as unimportant as a needy client interrupt (remember the market trader in *Monty Python's Life of Brian*, who insisted on haggling despite having a first, outrageous price accepted?).

I've read that on average, salespeople miss two and a half buying signals before they actually twig that the client wants to buy. I've no idea how this figure was arrived at, but it doesn't surprise me.

I also suspect that male salespeople are worse at spotting buying signals than females. Women often make excellent salespeople, contrary to the myth that you have to be aggressive and macho to sell, as usually they listen more carefully.

Classic buying signals:

★ The word 'need'. Obvious, but often overlooked. Remember that good selling is about creating win–win situations. These guys need X; you've got it.

★ Even more magical is 'need' plus 'now'. I've been told by prospects 'your timing is excellent', by which they mean I'm extremely lucky. When you receive these golden buy signals, remember that you are in the business of creating long-term relationships; restrain any instinct to drive a hard bargain with an obviously needy client. Drive a fair bargain, of course, but remember that next time round the boot might be on the other foot.

★ Other magic words. 'Problem', 'issue', 'difficulty', 'bottle-neck' – any conversation about what the client is finding a headache is excellent news for the salesperson, who is effectively being asked: 'Can you help us with this, please?' Remember the entrepreneur's magic question: 'Where's the pain?' It's a salesperson's magic question, too.

★ Complaints about your rivals' products/service/delivery (etc). As I've said, don't treat this as a chance to slag off your rival. Do treat it as an opportunity to explain how you can solve all these problems, starting today.

★ Any discussion of the buying process. These are often preceded by comments like, 'Of course, this is only in theory, but if we did decide to buy your X, how would we go about it?' The prospect has started to run a movie through their mind, where they buy your product, it solves the company's problems, they get kudos for it…

★ Objections. Novice salespeople are often put off by objections, but actually, these are a good thing, as they indicate interest. It's all part of this internal movie: like all good screenplays, there are complications that have to be dealt with. I talk more about handling objections below, but for now, the key thing is to realise their underlying positive import.

★ Good body language. Those barriers come down: the arms uncross, they lean forward, eye contact increases, they start mirroring your gestures. And of course, nothing beats the most basic 'body signal' of all, a smile. Clearly some purchasers will have poker skills – but not all do, and even the calm exterior of pros will crack if they sense you have just what they are looking for.

When you do get buying signals, act on them. If the customer expresses a need, reinforce it.

Customer: We need widgets badly.
Salesperson: Yes, there's a real shortage of good widgets at the moment.

And / or investigate it.

Customer: We need widgets badly.
Salesperson: Really? In what ways?

Don't belittle the need by promising an instant solution – it makes the customer look stupid.

At some point, however, you may wish to use the 'visualising question'.

Salesperson: 'So if I could offer you a way of solving your widget problems, I guess you'd be interested?'

The trouble with all these responses is that they can sound forced. If they do, they become an instant turn-off. It's better not to use them than to use them heavy-handedly – but better still to have them at the back of your mind, and use them, rephrased, at the right moment, in the right context. This is part of the professional skill of the hunter salesperson, a skill that you should never cease developing.

Handling objections

As I said, objections are often buying signals. The worst possible answer you can get when selling is a vague, 'Maybe…' If you get a clear no, you can ask why. It may be that they have misunderstood what you are saying.

No salesperson likes to think that they're no good at putting their point across, but often we are. And prospects aren't perfect listeners, either. Quite how they dare not hang on our every, wonderful word is a mystery, of course, but this can happen. Ensure that the prospect is saying no to you and what you have to offer, not to someone (s)he thinks you are, with a set of products (s)he thinks you have.

If there has been no misunderstanding, is the objection a 'dealbreaker' or something that can be negotiated around? Try and establish what the conditions behind the 'no' are. When you think you have uncovered them, feed them back to the prospect to make them explicit. 'So in six months' time, you will have a budget…' 'So if we could find a way of delivering these grommets to the North Pole, you would be interested…'

objections
are **often**
buying signals

Some standard objections, and how to meet them

We already get our stuff from XYZ

You should have known this before you went into the meeting, but you're here now… Ask what the prospect particularly likes about XYZ. If it is an area where you can match or beat them, say so. You will need an endorsement to prove your point, of course. You should know all your rivals, what their strengths are, and have arguments at hand to show you can beat them. If XYZ really are better than you, don't lie. Leave on a positive note: 'So, if we could deliver quicker than that, you'd be interested…' Never give in to 'dissing' XYZ.

▶▶

We have a contract with XYZ

'When does it come up for renewal?' Ask to bid. If you have a good relationship with the prospect, point out that your bidding would force some extra concessions out of XYZ, thus doing the prospect a favour. If you can use this to find out the terms of the contract, you have useful information.

We tried you before and were disappointed

Not a problem for the start-up, but often encountered by salespeople from established businesses. It is poor qualification on your part: you should have known this! Never mind, you're here now. Find out what went wrong, in as much detail as possible. Say that things have improved since then (and cite details of how these improvements came about – if there has been no improvement, don't lie!). The prospect may be curious to see if those idiots really have sorted themselves out…

It's not company policy to buy in this fashion

This is often a smokescreen. Is the person you are talking to the real decision maker? Probably best to look for alternative routes into the company.

I'd like to see a demo, but we haven't got time

Find a reference customer for whom your product has saved time. If the prospect carries on yes-butting, they are either lazy or not a decision maker.

You're too expensive

You should have your product fairly priced, so have you conveyed the real benefits it delivers? Run through them again. Remind the prospect that 'you get what you pay for'. Did he or she drive to work this morning in a Trabant? If price really is the issue, and nothing else (not reliability, quality, service etc), go away and rethink your offer.

A specific key person dislikes your company

Again, a problem for representatives of established businesses. Remedy it if you can. They may have misunderstood something or have memories of something done by people who have long ago left: the company is different now. If nothing can be done – at least you now know that. Can you find a way round this person?

⬤Beermat.biz

Much worse than an objection is indifference. 'Well, we might be interested but we're not sure…' Cast your minds back to those teenage years when you were trying to pair up with someone from the opposite sex. A clear 'no' – well, you knew where you stood. You could, if you liked, try and find out why, and maybe that's how you learnt that putting on three gallons of aftershave wasn't a brilliant idea after all. The worst thing was to be 'strung along'.

It still is.

Stringing along can happen for a number of reasons. It may be that the prospect doesn't want to hurt you by saying no – which is more often the case than you might think in the apparently 'hard' world of business, especially if you are, as we recommend, a likeable person. It maybe that he or she wants to keep options open – fine, as long as you establish that fact and don't waste time piling on sales effort (just keep the account on 'hold' and stay in touch). It may be that the prospect has been taught to act indifferent, as some purchasing directors are. It may be that you haven't qualified properly, and this isn't the right person to be talking to. It could be a psychological 'game', in which case you are being used...

How can you tell which of the above is the case? The easy answer is that you learn after a while. On the issue of psychological games, if you feel a sense of puzzlement after a meeting, you may well have been roped into one.

Whatever the reason, if after a couple of meetings you feel yourself no closer to a goal, something is amiss. If you can't pin it down to one of the above, you are best backing off, anyway, and expending your efforts elsewhere.

The answer the salesperson and the lonely teenager wants, is, of course, 'yes!' It rarely jumps out of the blue: you have to work towards it by closing.

Low-hanging fruit

Prospects who say 'yes' quickly are the *low-hanging fruit* dreamt of by all salespeople. And such people do exist. Most markets are made up of prospects with more or less 'pain' and more or less willingness and/or capacity to spend money on sorting that pain. My old friend, Graham Michelli, works on a rule of thumb that one third of the market is ready to buy if you present your case well, one third is impossible to budge and the other third is somewhere in between. Your job is to find out who the 'in pain, willing and able to sort it' third are, as quickly as possible, then to convince them that you are the people to do the job.

Note that the low-hanging fruit are not always the obvious ones. If they were, the whole process would be a lot easier. Few things can be more frustrating than trying to sell to a prospect who clearly has a desperate need for what you have to offer, but is either blissfully unaware of the fact, or for some other reason will not deal with you.

The opposite to this is the customer who doesn't seem to you to have a desperate need, but will try your product anyway. This may well be because they like you, or because they understand the market better than your researchers and better than the obvious candidates for the product, or for some totally arbitrary reason like they have just been given

▶▶

a budget to spend. Do not quibble with fate; work with these people and enjoy doing so! Don't be like Groucho Marx and 'not want to join any club that would accept you as member'. Go with the flow: the market is usually wiser than you are.

Keep plugging away quietly at the 'perfect on paper but hell in practice' prospect, but put your real efforts into people who want to buy now. Once you have reference customers and word begins to spread in the marketplace, the door of the difficult prospects may fly open. Or they may stay shut: maybe they have problems; maybe they have stopped keeping up with market changes. It is not your moral duty to rescue them from their foolishness.

Beermat.biz

Dealing with rejection

'No means no' can feel hurtful, especially for non-salespeople forced by circumstances to perform a sales role. But you have to learn to handle this. Natural sales people are lucky: they're thick-skinned and just bob off to the next opportunity. Other folk have to develop strategies to deal with this.

Some pointers:

★ **Have someone to talk to about it**. This is especially true for sole traders, who are very often exactly the people forced by circumstances to sell. Have a support network of confidants – your mentor, your partner, friends, a therapist or 'life-coach'.

★ **Remember, it wasn't personal**. This is hard, because selling *is* about personality and rapport. But it is also about business, and most rejections come because the prospect doesn't feel the pain strongly enough to want to spend money on it, or is already spending money with someone else. In those cases, even if someone with the charm of David Niven, the ethics of Mother Theresa, the intellect of Stephen Hawking and the looks of Richard Gere or Julia Roberts had been attempting the sale, they still wouldn't have got it.

★ **And if it was personal**... Sometimes, however, a meeting can end up with real antipathy. It's important to give yourself a boost after that. Some small, childish part of us wants to be liked by everybody, even though as adults we know this is not realistic (unless you're Will Rogers). If you are happy with your own conduct in the meeting and the other person played 'mindgames', then they are the one with the problem. Talk about it with your support network; learn; move on. As you network with fellow seekers for business, you can bet it won't be long before someone says, 'Have you met that awful buyer at Megacorp...?' Don't get into the demonising game, but do have a laugh about it.

★ **Use the experience to learn**. Non- or novice salespeople often lose sales by making simple 'technical' mistakes like failing to spot buying signals. Successful salespeople (and successful people generally) don't agonise about mistakes; when they run over them in their mind, it is to learn the lesson and conclude: 'I won't do that again!'

★ **Remind yourself of past successes**. Think back to times when you were welcomed by a customer and made a good sale. It'll be like that again.

★ **Get back on your horse**. Get selling again straight away. If it's been a particularly unpleasant knock, call your favourite customer and set up a meeting.

★ If you get **a run of bad luck** – remember, it happens to everybody. Let it make you pause, but not stop. Remember that the law of averages condemns even the best salespeople to runs of bad luck. And follow all the advice above, especially talking to people. No doubt you will soon hear they have had similar misfortunes and bounced back, stronger as a result.

Rejection can be particularly irksome if it's from a prospect that looked 'perfect on paper' (see above). Don't worry – get back on the hunt for that low-hanging fruit.

Time management

Overarching all the above techniques is the topic of *time management*. When I started working in the technology sector – yes, I escaped from the scaffolding business – I often found myself talking to people who were fascinated by the new gizmo I was selling. They weren't trying to steal information; they were simply interested. Because I put no small, incremental closes in the procedure, I kept on discussing stuff, organising demonstrations and technical talks – until the time came to ask for money, at which point the 'prospect' smiled and said that he had no money for this kind of thing. 'But it's fascinating, Mike. Do show me how the software works again…'

Good salespeople are masters of the art of speeding up the sales process. Not to rush people into an unwanted sale, which is contrary to the Beermat ethic, but to cut wasted time.

The sanity check (see page 103) is a key tool for either speeding things up or, if there is a fixed timetable (as is often the case for large, formal contracts), for finding out if you are a genuine contender for the job or just going through the dreadful palaver of 'beauty parades', shortlists etc to make up numbers. Naturally, if the latter is the case, you want to spend as little time and energy on the project as possible.

Time management is also about geography. Are you wasting your time making excessively long journeys between meetings? I advise companies to have a map in a very prominent place, with pins in for key prospects and customers. It gives a clear visual image of how they are faring, as well as helping salespeople avoid mad dashes from one side of town (or the UK, or the world) to another.

Chapter Six: The Sales Process 1 – Lift-Off

This chapter is about sales in the start-up: how you get the whole process moving. (The 'you' addressed in this chapter is the sales cornerstone of that start-up.) Established businesses might consider using the techniques outlined below to give stale sales efforts a fresh boost.

As Julie Andrews said, let's start at the very beginning…

The product

Two big questions. First, *is it right for the market?*

A perfectly fair answer for the start-up is that you have no idea. 'I think it's brilliant, but I'm just about to find out whether anyone else does – by selling to them.' But you can give yourself the best chance possible by getting your elevator pitch right. (Right *for now*: your elevator pitch may change as you find out who really wants the product and why.) Remember the material from the Beermat box…

First is the *elevator pitch* – a brief summary of exactly what it is you do, for whom, and why should they buy it from you. Ask the *magic question:* 'Where's the pain?' Where are customers incurring cost, waste and inefficiency? Where are they missing opportunities, getting lousy service, having to search hard for information, losing their own customers (etc)?

◖Beermat.biz

Have you really thought this through? Not just 'what you do', but 'for whom'? Where, among individuals or sectors with money to spend and which you know you can reach, is the pain most intense and intractable? This is the question of *focus*.

Some people have a very clear idea of their focus: 'This is for vets'; 'This is for people living within a ten mile radius of Dewsbury.' Others don't, and this is reasonable – as long as you understand that you have to find a focus pretty quickly. Get networking; make some early sales; see what patterns emerge; follow these. What is not permissible is to say 'they're for everybody' and ignore actual buying patterns that emerge.

The question 'why from you?' is often ignored, too. I meet many people who say they are setting up a web-based services company. I ask why they will be different from the thousands of other similar companies, and they often have no real answer, other than to say they're good at what they do. No doubt, but are their rivals incompetent fools?

This is *differentiation*. It's an old adage that to get people to switch to your business, you have to be ten per cent cheaper, better, easier or nicer. Which one are you? Everybody likes to think 'better', but are you? Really? We advise people to avoid 'cheaper' (see my comments below). So it's 'easier' or 'nicer' for many, many businesses. Which is fine, as we all live in a locality, so can be easier to reach than some faceless, far-away company. And we're all nice, aren't we? Beermat companies make it their business to be nice.

Another useful pointer for getting the product right is 'think service'. This is not a new idea – it all started back in the Sixties, when Theodore Levitt challenged manufacturers by asking, 'What business are you really in?' Cars or 'getting people from A to B'? The latter, of course. However entrepreneurs, especially ones entranced by technology, still regularly lose sight of this fact. Don't. All good businesses are there to solve particular customer pain, and this is rarely achieved by simply handing over a gadget or a bundle of software.

Also, customers think differently when negotiating about services than when they are negotiating for things. Things are more like 'commodities' and can turn quite mild-mannered individuals into ruthless bargainers. But nobody wants to get services on the cheap, in case they turn out to be exactly that: cheap and bad.

Businesses with a high service content are easier to expand, too. You don't have to worry about bottlenecks the way a manufacturer does, who at some time has to think: 'Do we need to build a whole new plant to meet rising demand?'

Whenever anyone comes to me with a new product they want me to sell, I always brainstorm with them the idea: 'How could we sell this as a pure service?' Supposing we gave the gizmo away free, could we build a business out of it? The results are often very illuminating.

Then I turn the tables: 'How could we sell this for double the price you're planning to charge?' More service ideas usually follow from this.

Established businesses eager to pep up their sales would do well to follow the same process.

cheaper, better, *easier* or **nicer**

The second big question is, *is the product correctly priced?*

At the very start of the life of an innovative product, the answer is probably that you haven't a clue. Everything is ultimately worth what a critical mass of customers are prepared to pay for it, but, especially for start-ups with new technology, nobody knows what this figure is.

Establish a ballpark estimate. If your product saves cost, how much does it save? Or if it is a manufactured product, you could work out your own cost and add on a margin, but beware of underestimating costs of after-sales service: you don't want to end up having to compromise on this to break even. Look around at similar products – entrepreneurs are often excessively optimistic about how unique their product is – and see what they charge and, most important, why they charge it. Could you charge the same? Could you charge more?

If you have a potential customer who is prepared to be your mentor, ask them outright how much they would pay to get rid of the pain your product solves.

Failing that, try the 'gold, silver and bronze' approach once you get in front of prospects.

'We actually offer three services. Gold is £50,000; silver is £5,000, bronze is £500.'

Have case histories to hand. If the product is new, then you'll have to make them up. Don't pretend they are real, just say they are examples of the level of service you intend to offer. Make each offer as compelling as the other: remember that the customer is not buying *your* work but a solution to *their* problem, so gold must solve at least £50,001 worth of pain. The answer you get will tell you a lot about how much different people have to spend.

This is not the same as having a formal price list. They may, for example, say 'something between the silver and the gold', which is an infuriating answer if you already have those products lined up, but excellent information if you are really still trying to establish what the market will bear.

Finally, remember that competing on pure price is hell, unless you can radically undercut the opposition with a new way of stripping cost out of your process, the way the budget airlines have done (business-school types call this a 'disruptive technology', though it often isn't so much technology that does the disrupting as a redefinition of what customers actually want). People aren't that fussed about saving a few pence, especially in services. They are very fussed about (and expect) quality; they like ease and niceness.

If you are in 'commodity hell', you must find a differentiator. Go back to the brainstorm I talked about earlier and ask: 'How could I add service to justify being the most expensive product on the market?' If nothing useful emerges from this, life is going to be tough.

Your first sale

This will probably be to someone you know, or a contact provided by the business's mentor. They will probably buy because they like you, and because the product looks potentially interesting – and because you offer a good deal. Never give anything away free, as free stuff never gets respected, but do expect to transact very early sales on unfavourable terms. What you are getting is a foot in the door, a potential customer mentor and the chance to test the product in the real world.

How do you make such a sale? Everyone in the team should trawl their personal networks for potential early customers. It will then be the job of the sales cornerstone to get the sales process moving as soon as possible. The route will probably be:

★ Team brainstorming session – who does any of us know who would benefit from our product? (Involve your business's mentor in this discussion.)

★ Whoever has the contact gets in touch with them…

★ …and puts them in touch with the sales cornerstone (or, if the team lacks a sales cornerstone, whoever is in charge of sales. But get a proper cornerstone quick!)

★ Introductory meeting between sales cornerstone and prospect

★ Secondary meeting leading to 'mini-sale' (see page 105)

★ Successful delivery of 'mini-sale'

★ Any further meetings – as few as possible – needed to get a full deal

Or you may leap straight over the mini-sale to a deal – we did, at The Instruction Set, selling a £20,000 training course to a

Swedish contact of mine the morning after we'd founded the company. We then, of course, had to write the course. In true start-up fashion, we managed it at the last moment. I remember sitting in our basement office sticking course materials into binders, with one eye on the clock as the flight to Stockholm was leaving that afternoon. But we made it to the airport, and the course was a big success.

Remember that in Beermat methodology, the first sale (and the next few sales, too) are of a highly provisional product. The course we gave in Sweden went down well, but there were a number of omissions, which my client pointed out to me when I talked through the sale after it had been delivered. I relayed these comments back to the rest of the team, and the delivery cornerstone made changes to the course in the light of them.

Once the sale has gone through – not 'once the money is safely in the bank', but once the customer has taken delivery and is satisfied – it is time to write the White Paper. A reminder of what I said on page 7...

What was it like for the customer? How did they actually use the product? What did they find particularly helpful? What did they dislike or end up not using? How could it be improved? This will help the business refine the product, as well as the elevator pitch and its understanding of the real market it is in. The sales cornerstone will oversee the writing of this paper, getting input from technical and financial specialists.

Beermat.biz

The White Paper has a range of uses. It focuses the technical team on producing the improvements that are desired by the client, rather than those driven by their own curiosity. For the client, it shows the start-up's seriousness of intent: the aim is to build a long-term, mutually beneficial relationship. For the sales cornerstone it provides the basis of a sales document.

The next few sales

The more your first customer will act also as a customer mentor, the better – which is why such a person is best found among people you already know and like. As such, they will provide personal referrals, or at least an endorsement.

But at the same time, keep using your network to find customers. The job is easier now you have a real, satisfied customer, and a White Paper (or a version of it, written up as a positive case history, to tell their story).

The kind of deal you should strike is similar to your first one – you still need mentoring, credibility and the chance to try things out more than you need to drive a hard bargain. If you can, write White Paper-style reports of each sale.

This is all part of the 'virtuous circle of product development and market discovery' I referred to earlier. For the alert, energetic company, of course, this circle is unending, but it is at its most intense at the start of the business's life.

After a while, you should have a much clearer view of the business basics. the actual pain you solve, for whom, and why you are the right organisation to deliver it. You should also have a better idea of what you can charge for it. It may be that discrete groups of customers appear, with differing pains which are solved by the product. If so, you have several markets, which makes life more complex, but possibly more exciting too.

As important as that is the actual portfolio of customers – individuals, not organisations. Is one – or better, are some – of them shaping up to be a customer mentor? Try and bring this about.

After that, the product(s) need to 'settle'. Once the team has come to, and shares, a clear view of the basics, you have to harden your heart a little. Every customer will want something a bit different, and many salespeople are too eager to please: a fault in the right direction, but a fault nonetheless. If *every* customer wants their widgets blue rather than red but your techies prefer red, it is the sales cornerstone's duty to insist the customer gets blue. If *one* customer wants blue, the cornerstone must check with the rest of the team that blue is technologically possible and financially viable before promising it.

Naturally for some, 'big ticket' products, total customisation will always be a part of the offer. But for most products it can't be.

No first sale

I sometimes get asked, 'What can I do if I can't find any potential customers among my contacts?'

One answer is 'panic', but it's not one I would give.

I worry about any entrepreneur who uses 'I' the whole time. Business is a team game: *everybody in the team* should be looking through their address books or PDAs for potential customers. If they, collectively, can't find one, I have to wonder if they are in the right business. However, if they assure me that they are, that their product really will solve pain and that they really can deliver it better (or nicer, or easier, or radically cheaper) than anyone else, then my answer is twofold.

One, and most important, is to get networking. Find potential customers, now!

You can also resort to a more structured sales methodology. Ideally this is something you only do once you have been round the 'first sale – white paper – several more sales – product and market understood' loop outlined above. But if you really do believe in what you have, but for some reason can't find a first customer however hard you try, you might as well leap straight ahead to the structured model outlined in the next chapter. You will have to phrase your Beermat intro email rather differently, as you lack a reference customer (don't make one up; head the email with the key benefit you think you are bringing and adapt the rest of the template on page 91 intelligently). But in my view this is a tough route. Are you really sure you know what you are doing? Have at least one pub session where the team brainstorm alternatives to the offer for which you can't find any customers.

An unusual, but not unheard-of, variation on the above is the phenomenon where a business gets one customer but can't get any more. Ask for a meeting with that customer. Is there enough chemistry between you to make them want to be a fully-fledged customer mentor? If not, at least try and get an endorsement out of them, for your intro email.

Both the above scenarios can happen, but it is much more likely that your business will get customers. Well done! Time to move on.

Chapter Seven: The Sales Process 2 – Creating Momentum

You have a clear view of what pain your product solves, and a number of successful sales under your belt. How do you begin accelerating the sales process?

There are two ways. One is classic Beermat sales. Your people are networking furiously, and an endless stream of personal contacts comes in as a result, a decent proportion of which turn into sales. Not only this, but happy customers are also networking: word gets round that what you have to offer is excellent, so people are actually contacting you out of the blue. Some by direct referral, others via your website.

Such an outcome is hugely worth striving for, especially if you are in a small marketplace where it is perfectly possible to know all the key players. Keep networking! All of you!

But for the vast majority of sapling start-ups and established one-person businesses, partnerships and SMEs, it is necessary to have a more structured model of lead generation running *alongside* the networking model.

The balance you strike between the two methods is up to you. I really can't lay down the law, here, as every business is different. As a very rough rule, the larger the 'ticket' of the sale, the smaller and more intimate the market, the newer the product, and the more service-oriented the product, the more you should rely on networking and avoid the formal method outlined below. But that is a generalisation, and I'm sure bright readers will come up with exceptions. Arguably a better answer is simply to try both, and see which ends up working best.

The initial list

The structured approach begins with a list of prospects.

You can buy such lists. People selling them claim they are 'pre-qualified', in other words that everyone on it has expressed an interest in a certain kind of product. However they are not always up-to-date. I recently heard about one list, being used by a major company, on which several of the contact names were not only no longer in business but actually dead. Even if you know a list to be up-to-date, you don't know how many other people have been sold it, too. Buyers of lists often start calling and get a reply along the lines of, 'Oh, God, not another one…'

If there is a well-established *directory* – most areas of business have a market-leading directory that is regularly updated and in which the main players want to be mentioned – you'd be better off buying that and doing the qualification yourself.

Other ways of building lists include surfing the Internet, looking through the phone book or, as some entrepreneurs I know have done, driving round trading estates noting down company names.

Qualifying the list: data versus information

Your next task is to bring this list to life. At its most basic, this means getting the name and contact details (phone, email address) of the person in each prospect organisation with power to order your product. Sometimes this is easy: 'Who's in charge of buying your widgets?' will do the job – though see the box on the terrors of Ebenezer Scrooge below. Other times you have to be a bit more subtle.

Good telemarketers go beyond this, however. They don't just gather *data* but *information*. I define information as data that gets behind the official face of an organisation and tell you what's really going on. This will be hugely useful when you start approaching them.

A sympathetic telemarketer can sometimes get enormous amounts of information by chatting to the person on the other end of the line. What's business like? Is this Mr Bloggs approachable or not? This is why I say that sales naturals are best for this job.

Efficiency freaks demotivate the best telemarketers by tying them down to tight schedules, call-centre style. Wrong. Let them chat. Even trivial facts can turn into information in the right context: knowing that it's raining in Wakefield at the moment may not be information; knowing that it's like that every autumn and there's still nowhere you can buy decent umbrellas might well be.

Of course, the chatty approach doesn't always work. Some companies have a 'no-name' policy and enforce it strictly. Good telemarketers are thick-skinned enough to deal with the rejection; they simply put a cross against the company name and move on to the next one.

Avoiding the professionals

Professional purchasers in big companies are taught to negotiate hard with professional salespeople. If you are a sole trader, SME or start-up, you'd rather avoid this Scrooge-like individual. But his is the contact name your telemarketer will most likely be given when he or she phones up…

This is one of the reasons why selling via personal networking is easier than through a formal methodology. Through a network you may well meet managers who have first-hand experience of the pain your product can solve, and a small budget they can spend on solving that pain. You can befriend that person, sell them as much 'pain solving' as he or she can sign off, deliver superbly, then get them on your side, as a customer mentor. Get them to introduce you round the organisation – and past Mr Scrooge.

The alternative can be nasty. One entrepreneur we worked with was nearly bankrupted because he did an appallingly one-sided deal with a global soft-drink company, giving him microscopic margins and snail-like payment terms.

Morally, it is no excuse for Ebenezer and his corporate employers to say, 'Well, that's business.' To maximise long-term value from small companies, big ones need to cultivate and help them along: bullying and machismo don't help this.

▶▶

I'm afraid I have no magic answer for this. Some thoughts:

Your *telemarketers* should be aware of the need to avoid professional purchasers, and instead try to find out the names of managers most afflicted by the pain your product solves. This is a much harder task than just getting the name of the head of purchasing – which is why you need good telemarketers.

Secondly, this highlights the need for a *proper sales cornerstone* rather than someone else in the team 'trying his or her hand at a bit of sales'. A professional purchaser will eat the latter for breakfast. A proper sales cornerstone – who, remember, is a sales natural – will be a much fairer match. (Even a sales cornerstone recruited via the 'find a natural then teach them to sell' route will do better than a non-sales person. If they make a mess of the first few encounters, they will learn their new, chosen craft fast.) Those sales virtues – charm, persistence, intelligence – will come into their own.

Thirdly, remember that the purchaser will not get brownie points if he shoos away someone with a product which is then taken up by his employer's deadly rival and saves them a million pounds in its first year. Have a *brilliant product,* and even the most misanthropic purchaser will have to take you seriously. You might end up finding he has a nicer side – especially at Christmas…

⌐Beermat.biz

There are other ways of gaining information about a prospect. You do have broadband Internet access, don't you? If not, rush out and get it now. If you are in a company without it, find some way of getting it, even if it means blackmailing the boss…

A look at a *company website* can tell you a lot about the business. How does it see itself? How does it wish to be seen by others? Has it put its mission statement on the net? Read it. Skim through the press releases. Companies put these on the net in the fond dream that the world will log on and be amazed. It won't, but you, as a potential supplier, can gain a lot of information from them.

Trade magazines are another source of information. However obscure a sector you are planning to sell to, there'll be a mag for it, as viewers of *Have I Got News For You?* know. Read this publication thoroughly – and keep it once you've read it: you are building a library. Cross-reference your library if you can; if you really can't face doing that, consider paying someone else to do so. But doing your own cross-referencing is a good discipline: you will remember odd news items about particular companies if you are the one keeping the records. Note the names of the regular feature writers, too. They will probably be freelances who have become experts on the subject over the years. Can you get to know them? If you can use that natural, salesperson likeability to persuade them to join you for lunch, then do so – on you; it's a great investment.

Add to your library anything you see in the *papers*, local or national. I've had mixed fortunes with press-cutting agencies. Some people recommend them as sources of prospect information, but I find them inefficient: you get sent (and charged for) too much irrelevant stuff. The time for one of these agencies is when you are beginning to get noticed, and you want to find out what other people are saying about *you*.

Work with your *mentor* on your list. He or she may well also have comments to make about specific prospects.

Make sure you structure the reward system for your telemarketers to encourage them to provide information, not just data.

How big should the initial list be? I believe in starting slowly, so aim to have around one hundred qualified prospects at the end of the process. You can always have another trawl if there are obviously more potential buyers out there.

Securing the first meeting

You should now have a list of prospects with:

★ Correct contact details

★ An individual whom you have reason to believe has 'power to order' (if possible, and it may not be possible, not the purchasing director)

★ At least one piece of information about the company

So begin to close. Very slowly, almost invisibly, start making the prospect do something for you – in this case, write a time for a meeting into their diary and then actually be there when you turn up for it. It's not a huge amount to ask, but enough to weed out a large number of future non-customers.

Naturally, you want to get as many of these fifteen-minute meetings as possible. How do you do this?

The answer is through *email*. The phone is an inflexible medium, adequate for gathering information but not really up to the subtle task of securing time with someone you don't know. Letters are actually better – or were, before email killed them: unsolicited letters now almost always end up 'filed' in the bin. Emails are not intrusive, as the phone is; unlike letters, they have a good chance of getting read, unless they are spam or personal but verbose. Spam is illegal in some situations, and never a good way for a serious business to announce itself to the world. You will write a very specific kind of introductory email: compelling, brief and personal (every email will be slightly different, written individually and sent to a specific person).

The Beermat introductory email (aka Mike's Magic Email)

There are five key aspects to this – which translate into four *brief* paragraphs plus the all-important subject heading.

1 *'I notice…'* Use your information here. 'I noticed that Acme have recently overtaken MidiCorp as the largest suppliers of grommets in the UK…' Or personal information: 'Congratulations on your appointment as COO of MicroCorp…'

Note that if someone has 'just been appointed…' they may well be interested in replacing incumbent suppliers. Whenever, in your regular trawl of the web/specialist press, you find a new appointment in the right area, drop them a Beermat intro email, just to let them know who you are and how good you are.

2 *Your elevator pitch.* The basic benefit you deliver. Remember the Magic Question: where's the pain? Why does this company need your product/service now? 'We believe we can cut your costs by twenty-five per cent.'

3 The *proof.* By far the best proof is a personal endorsement by somebody highly respected in the industry. Such people exist in every industry – if you're already in it, you'll know who they are; if you're trying to break in, look at the trade press and talk to your mentor. If you are new-ish to the industry but have a few customers, one of them will tell you who to contact.

Failing that, use an existing customer, even if he or she is in a relatively obscure company. No, that is not as good as having a recognised 'maven' (see page 131) pronounce on your business, but it still puts you ahead of anybody making unsubstantiated claims.

4 Finally, of course, you ask for a *meeting*. Always offer to visit the customer – it takes less of their time, but also gives you an invaluable chance to take a peek at their organisation. Is it buzzing or half-asleep? Suggest a general time, 'week commencing June 3rd' for example.

5 The *subject heading*. A well-written email will get you a long way, but it is no use if nobody opens it. For all I know the one I received yesterday from fneij590djr09ejf9 offering me cheap Viagra (Chris, who lives in East Anglia, gets deluged with emails offering to sell him septic tanks) may have been an offer I really could not have refused. But I didn't open it.

Your Beermat intro email will have an arresting subject heading. If you have a personal endorsement from a respected industry player, that's the ideal one: 'Recommendation from Joanna Smith'. The recipient will spot the name and open the mail. (Of course, you *must* check with your endorser that they are happy to be used in this way. It is a step beyond a simple endorsement, and they may not agree.)

If this option is unavailable, then revert to your information. 'Heard the news about Midicorp.' 'Congratulations on your appointment.' The generic 'save money on widgets' is best avoided – you can do better than that! – and of course you won't be using those things that spam filters pick up, like sentences beginning with Free, CAPITALS, loads of exclamation marks!!! But you weren't planning to send something like that, anyway, were you?

Model Beermat intro email

Subject: Referral from Joanna Smith

cc.   Joanna Smith

Dear Mr Jones,

I noticed from your website that HyperCorp just won the Department of Ag and Fish national flange contract. Congratulations!

Joanna suggested I get in touch, as we do all the flange design for MegaCorp.

Joanna would be pleased to provide a reference: joanna.smith@megacorp.com

I'd like to arrange a short meeting. I will be in Neasden on Tuesday 14th in the morning. Can you spare me fifteen minutes?

Regards

Mike Southon

Acme Flange Design

Beermat.biz

Though the end product looks deceptively simple, it can take time to craft the Beermat intro email. This is time well spent. In one of the software companies I have worked for, we developed a product that we knew would be of huge value to insurance companies. At the time, insurers still assessed items in any property portfolio they were quoting for by postcode, whereas our technology allowed them to do so by exact location, all on computer, of course. It would save (and is now saving) them millions. However, they still needed to be told this fact, and convinced of it.

Luckily, we already had a major customer in the sector; and luckier still, he was happy to endorse the product. So we drew up a list of the one hundred top insurance companies, put a telemarketer on to the case qualifying this list, and ended up with names of particular individuals to contact and, in some cases, some information about the companies. Then I sat down to write the email.

time spent **crafting** the **Beermat email** …is time **well spent**

First priority – a customer referee. Sorted.

Second priority – a real understanding of how our product would help the clients. Where was their pain? The answer was risk – always a good hook for the insurance business. By only being able to assess by postcode, they were using an excessively rough guide to risk.

Once these were established, it was a matter of turning these two key points into specific emails for the one hundred people at the one hundred companies we had selected. It took time, but we were finally ready to send them off.

Salespeople familiar with direct mail will know that anything over a one-per-cent reply rate is good – I have seen dismal direct mail campaigns to which nobody at all has replied. Cold calling can get a five-per-cent success rate, if brilliantly done. Our mail to one hundred people got twelve replies, several of whom subsequently turned into customers (one *Sales on a Beermat* attendee recently trumped this, getting twenty-six appointments from a mailout to two hundred local authorities).

When you have sent your email, wait a couple of weeks to see what happens. Then contact all non-repliers. Strange as it may seem, the best way to do this is to simply resend the original. This is because the most likely reason for the recipient's failing to reply is either that they read the email, made a note to do something about it, then got distracted by other things; or that they missed it altogether (and will thus assume this is the first time you have been in contact). Either way, a simple resend won't be taken as rude.

The big fear, that someone will accuse you of spamming, is not based on reality. The chances of this happening are remote: these emails are not spam, because they are composed for, and addressed to, an individual. (If, despite this assurance, you are still worried about being accused of spamming, phone the company and ask the person's PA for permission to email them.)

People who send emails correctly are rarely accused of spamming. If such an accusation is made (and you have followed my rules), the accuser is wrong. However don't make a fuss: it's best to simply apologise and delete the person from your list. They are almost undoubtedly time-wasters. But still say 'sorry' to them, at which point they will be satisfied and will go off and annoy someone else.

A subset of first-time non-responders will reply to this second email. For those that don't, wait another few weeks then call them on the phone. Some will be unavailable and not return calls; others will talk with you but say they are not interested. But a proportion will have been aware of the emails and will have a real interest.

For those who vanish – let them go. Contact them again once you have something new to say.

Email on a Beermat

★ Never spam

  • Individual recipient

  • No multiple addresses

★ Headings in lower case, no silly punctuation

★ Brief

★ Closed questions

  • Inviting yes/no or a simple piece of information

★ Simple format

★ No attachments

Beermat.biz

Any other hints about email? Don't send mails in a fancy format that looks like it might be a virus (such as those emails on headed notepaper). And avoid attachments wherever possible: they clog up the email boxes of big email users, who are wary of them anyway because they might contain viruses, for example via one of those worms that gets into people's address books and sends out emails that purport to come from the victim. If someone contacts you with a request for further information about your business, don't reply with an attachment but a weblink to the most relevant page on your site. Only if actually asked for a specific document should you send attachments.

avoid
attachments

I, and people I teach, use the Beermat intro email a lot, and it usually works well. When it doesn't work, there are always good reasons. The main ones are:

Irrelevant endorser. The person endorsing the product, or at least the company for whom they work, should ideally be known (by reputation anyway) to the recipient. If they are not – for example in a very fragmented industry – this can be a problem. Talk to your mentor about finding someone with more clout.

Feature sell. All sales books make this point, but people keep on making the same mistake, so I'll join in the chant. Is the 'benefit' you highlighted in your second paragraph really a benefit to the company, or just a feature that sounds fun? Think of things from their point of view. Where's their pain? Not just a slight ache, but real pain. Excessive cost and miserable customers are two great places to look. If you can quantify the pain relief (with a sensible degree of accuracy), all the better.

Too long. A Beermat email is brief. If yours was too long, the recipient's heart sank on opening it: they probably skim-read the first line or two to see if it was from someone they knew, then deleted it.

Wrong moment. This is the most likely reason: the email just didn't get noticed. Certain industries are rushed off their feet at certain times of year, and quieter at others. They will have a cycle of delivery and recuperation (which includes doing things like renewing supplier contracts): contact them at the start of the latter. For every business, avoid August or Christmas. I find that the best times to send Beermat intro emails are about a week after major holidays, i.e. the second week in January, the second week after Easter and the second week in September.

Look at all these possible ways of slipping up, and be honest about how your email measures up to them. If, on reflection, it fell into these traps, rewrite it. If you can, send it out to a different set of prospects.

If the amended email fails to elicit any response, you will have to face up to the likelihood that your offer does not have the magic you imagined.

Re-read the section on 'one sale only' in the previous chapter. Are you sure you know what your reference customer liked about what you did for them?

If you have no such customer, and have been sending out speculative emails – have a chat with your business mentor, but my advice in this situation is 'back to the pub'.

It is important to understand that the best salesperson in the world cannot sell a product nobody wants. I've had several unfortunate spells working on high-tech ideas which people simply wouldn't pay for. The first time this happened, I feared I had lost my touch as a salesman. Then I moved on to something else, and people I'd never even met were phoning me for it.

I believe that most new products fall into two categories: relatively easy winners, and losers. Customers either light up when an idea is put to them, or nod sagely and ask what else you have on offer. In the middle, of course, there are ideas which need extra work – and persistence – to get right.

For the sales cornerstone, trying to sell a 'loser' product should be a learning experience. As with all rejection, the best solution is to find something better to sell and get selling again it as soon as possible. There are plenty of entrepreneurs out there looking for good salespeople. Get networking! And be choosy.

The sales cornerstone may well decide the venture is flawed before the entrepreneur does. This can cause great upset. You, the sales cornerstone, will undoubtedly be accused of being a lousy salesperson. You have to look inside yourself, and be able to say that you did the best you could: in your professional judgement the product simply wouldn't sell. This can be tough: if a finance cornerstone gets a roasting for saying the product can't be manufactured profitably, they can point to figures. You have to rely on lists of calls and visits made, but that only protects you against accusations of idleness, not lack of skill.

If you are convinced that you did your best but nobody wanted the product, take the knock and leave. Maybe someone else with a different sales style will do a better job. Or maybe the product genuinely is a loser – in which case the entrepreneur will have to find out for themself.

Don't forget that the entrepreneur will suffer most from the failure. They need to learn all the lessons they can from 'what went wrong' and to move on to newer and more promising fields. You might be able to help them with that – when they are prepared to listen.

The worst thing of all is to keep plugging away at a clear loser.

Of course, I hope you will not be in this situation. Even if you get only one answer to your email, that could be all you need.

But let's not end on a negative note – this process is highly likely to generate leads, which you are now about to turn into real prospects.

Chapter Eight: The Sales Process 3 – From Prospect to Customer

Well done. You're not a loser, you've got a meeting – several meetings, actually – from a couple of referrals, from your Beermat intro email and from someone you met at a networking event. So get into positive mode; go in there and sell, sell, sell!

Whoa! Take a step back…

The fifteen-minute meeting

This first meeting will probably be largely about qualifying. There will, of course, be a small close at the end, but most of the time you will be listening and learning.

Don't rush into this meeting. You need to do more research. You took a look at the company website when qualifying the lead: now go back and take a longer look. Read all the press releases. Find out all you can about the key people in the business: what are their backgrounds, their stories, their main interests?

Use the net in other ways, too. Enter the company name on Google and see what comes up. Find chatrooms where the company's products are discussed. Get involved in the discussions yourself, anonymously of course.

Go through your library of trade papers and other collated information.

Become an expert.

This advice may sound ridiculous to businesses that rely on selling reasonably low-priced products/services to lots of customers. You haven't got the time to do all this stuff for a sale that might net you £500!

No, but the principle of 'learn as much as you can about a prospect before you meet them' still holds good. Pop on to the net and view their site. Look through your indexed library of information. Become as much of an expert as you can. And, of course, if this is an *early* sale, remember it isn't about money anyway, but about 'a foot in the door, a potential customer mentor and the chance to test the product in the real world'.

There is a particular attitude to take at the initial, fifteen-minute meeting. It's a strange (but achievable) mixture of confidence and humility. The *confidence* is in yourself and the product: 'I'm good; I'm here with something of value to the client; I'm the right person to be presenting it.' The *humility* is about the situation. 'The customer doesn't really know me or I them; even if he or she loves the idea, they may well have all sorts of internal hurdles to cross before we can make things happen. The usual negotiations lie ahead…'

Remember – 'listen and learn'. When you do speak, ask careful questions based on your research. What you have learned will help you judge the answers. Is the person you are dealing with being open with you? If you suspect they are not, challenge gently. 'I've heard the opposite…' 'There are rumours that…'

listen
and learn

And remember the importance of having an objective. In other words, do a tiny bit of closing. Precisely what this should be depends on the situation. Ideally, you need to establish:

★ if the prospect has a real need now (and, if not, whether such a need will arise in the near future and if so when, and whether they have other needs right now)

★ if the prospect has money to spend now (and, if not, whether and / or when they will have such money)

★ if they do have money now, roughly how much

★ if the person you have talked with has the power to spend that money (and if not, who does)

★ a future course of action

Of course, in a perfect world, you would not only learn all this, but sell at the first meeting. This is unlikely. In fact you'll be lucky to establish all five of the above. Minimum outcome? A clear answer to point five (future action) and progress on points one to four.

If the meeting simply reveals that the 'prospect' actually doesn't need what you've got and never will, or that they can't afford it and never will – be polite. I believe in the old maxim, 'What goes around, comes around.' You never know: the same person may move on to a needy, cash-rich company, or the company might suddenly hit gold… And there must be some piece of information about the market you can get from the encounter.

There are situations when people are rude – 'I've been asked to meet you, but I don't really want to, and we're not interested in what you have to sell…' Overcome your natural, healthy desire to biff them across their smug little face with your briefcase, and remember:

★ You now have the 'moral high ground'

★ You didn't come here to sell but to qualify. So ask questions. An interesting one might be why they were asked to meet you, and by whom. Another runs along the lines of, 'I'm obviously on the wrong track here. Can you suggest someone I should see?'

If someone is really offensive, then it's probably time to leave – but let your curiosity loose first. What's their problem?

The most likely outcome of a first meeting, however, is a qualified agreement. The prospect likes what you have to offer and thinks it's affordable – they'll get back to you.

Result!

Sorry, no. You must emerge from the meeting with concrete outcomes, not just interest and vague promises. If the prospect 'will get back to you', you must know *when* (and you must then hold him or her to that schedule). A real result is a promise of contact by a certain date plus the promise of another meeting with other, more senior people in the organisation.

After the fifteen-minute meeting, send an email along the lines of 'my understanding of what you need'. This shows you are serious and that you were listening during the meeting. If you misinterpreted something, you will be told – best to know

now, rather than later in the sales process. You can also add a nudge if necessary.

Secondary and tertiary meetings

These should follow. The golden rule is to up the stakes at each one – seeing someone more senior, getting closer to making an actual sale.

You must not get bogged down in an endless round of such meetings. Time for…

The sanity check

The hero of Franz Kafka's novel *The Castle* spends his days travelling towards the building in the title, and it just gets further and further away. Some sales efforts can become like this, especially in dealing with big companies. Up to a point you have to play this game (Kafka worked for a large insurance company and understood big organisations). But beyond that point, you do not have to play it, and should not play it, as your time is valuable. The big question is: 'Are they serious about doing business with me, but just going through their natural, convoluted purchasing process – or has something gone wrong?'

Things that can go wrong in the middle of the sales process include:

Fascinating technology. My problem when I started selling technology. Sadly, many 'techie' products fall into the unfortunate category of 'solutions in search of a problem', and doom people trying to make money out of them to the fate of Kafka's castle-seeking hero.

A lying individual. This happened to me. The circumstances are instructive: it was the first big deal for some software we had developed at The Instruction Set, so I was dealing with bigger companies than I was then used to. I found myself talking with a man who claimed to be the head of technology at a major corporation. He expressed great interest in our product, and we came to an office in their HQ and did a demonstration for him. Another meeting was organised, this time in a neutral meeting place which we paid for. A deal was nearly done then – he was going to clear things up with the CEO, and would get back to us on the phone. Which he did: the deal was on, provided we dropped our prices a bit. After some debate, we accepted this (we got a concession on payment terms in return), and he said a contract would be in the post. We began gearing ourselves up for delivery – but no contract arrived. After a week, I phoned the guy up, and asked what had happened to the contract. He said that he was a contractor, and was leaving on Friday.

Of course I should have qualified him better, earlier on. But I didn't, and he ran rings round me for weeks as a result.

You're a stalking horse. Companies like to put fear into their existing suppliers by flirting with someone new. Once they have quotes and a theoretical agreement from you, they wave this at the existing supplier, who then caves in to whatever demand the big company was making. You get told, 'Thank you very much for your interest but the business has gone somewhere else.'

There is not much you can do if this happens. The best you can make of it is that you have learned more about this company and made contacts there, and can keep selling to them in the future. They may feel they owe you for wasting your time – but they may not.

Internal politics. 'It was something to do with internal politics' (often accompanied with a shrug of cosmic bafflement) is the most common excuse used by poor salespeople when potential deals mysteriously wither away. In my view this is not a sufficient excuse. They should have qualified better, understood what was going on within the company, and done more to manage the process.

If you do find yourself stalled by internal politics, this is not an excuse for abandoning the sale, but an opportunity to find out more about the company. Who is doing the stalling and why? Can you get to them and change their mind? Time to put those sales personality traits of charm, persistence and intelligence to work…

In the interim period, the sale will have to be 'downgraded' on the Pipeline (see page 120), but don't give up.

People with nothing better to do. I genuinely think some companies organise complex procurement procedures for the hell of it. Or maybe for the power. Up to a point you have to put up with this, but only up to a point.

The keys to preventing all the above are good 'sanity checks' carried out as early as possible in the proceedings. There are three forms – if you can, apply them all.

1. The mini-sale. This is the best sanity check of all, and I recommend its use to anyone looking to do large-scale business. Can you sell the prospect some small, mini-version of what you do?

I have done lots of work for IT services companies, who are looking for long-term contracts worth tens of thousands of pounds. But my first sell to prospects is always a simple day of consultancy for around £500. The market breaks naturally into two segments: office managers who hate IT and want IT problems taken away; and IT professionals who hate everyone else in the business, and want all their petty complaints to go away (so they can get on with fun, techie stuff). I have a 'mini-product' for each of these archetypal customers: a day helping the office managers with their biggest problems (and teaching them how to solve them again if there's any time left), and a day doing dull 'grunt' work for the techies.

It always happens that several prospects who have expressed vague interest in a long-term deal won't even sign up for the one-day product, which makes me think they are hardly serious about taking us on full-time. Others take up the day, say, 'Thanks that was great,' but don't want anything else. In both cases you have saved a lot of time chasing a big deal that was never going to happen. Others, of course, like the day and ask about a more permanent contract.

Note that there is a benefit to the prospect, too, of your using this kind of sanity check. They get a chance to look at your work. Obviously you will be putting 'best foot forward', but it will still give them material on which to judge you. If I were awarding a large contract, I'd get all interested suppliers to do some small piece of work for me – for a fair rate – and see which ones I liked best, both personally and in terms of quality.

For both of you, there is the benefit that a relationship has begun to develop. Prospects may seem like termagants when they are grinding their way through selection procedures, but these can be irksome for them too (unless the person in charge is a power freak): knowing, liking and trusting a potential supplier actually makes their job easier.

I have heard people object that a £500 consultancy day shows the prospect you can deliver £500 consultancy days, not large projects. If handled with any kind of flair, the mini-sale shows you are serious about what you do, offer value for money and do so in a pleasant manner. It means they are more likely to trust you when you say you can deliver a bigger project.

ª relationship
has **begun**
to develop

2. A financial check. This should be carried out by your finance cornerstone, into the financial state of the prospect. Thank God, this is not a salesperson's job, but you are still in charge of the sale overall, so make sure this gets done.

If the prospect's finances look rocky, this is not necessarily a deal-killer, but it means you will have to watch payments like a hawk. In my view, it is right to be open about this. There's nothing sneaky about doing a financial sanity check; it is correct business practice. If it reveals cracks, talk this through with the prospect. If they get defensive and deny they have any problems, then you will have to walk away. The prospect should say: 'Things are rocky at the moment, but we're doing X, Y and Z to pull through.' One of those things is taking you on, and using the value you will add to their business to help them out of whatever mess they are in.

At the same time, with such clients be very clear about your credit terms and your procedures for what happens if payments dry up. Don't do so in a threatening manner – if anything, be apologetic. Be clear, friendly and firm.

3. The headed notepaper close. This is particularly useful when discussing big contracts. Once you have worked out the rough details of the sort and scale of work you will be doing if you win the business, ask for some confirmation of that, in writing, on company notepaper.

The document states what work the prospect wants done and that you are being considered for the job. The phrase 'subject to contract' can be added, to ensure the document is in no way legally binding. It is, nonetheless, a clear intent. It will weed out the kind of time-waster I encountered in my software story, and also serve to focus everyone's attention on what everybody is aiming for: a win-win outcome.

When the deal is a smaller one, a 'heads of agreement' should be drawn up as soon as possible, outlining (from the prospect) the work that needs doing, and from you how you intend to do it. Such a document should be produced later in the process if the contract is large, as a kind of 'second-line sanity check', to keep the prospect aware of your seriousness of intent.

If the sanity checks are positive, then it will be time to move on to the next phase of the process. Or rather to a set of phases – beauty parades, shortlists and so on – which I call the 'wasteland'. Nobody, except the very naïve who have not been through them before, or the incredibly worldly who know the outcome in advance, enjoys these phases, but for certain types of contract, such as large-scale government work, they have to be endured.

Do everything you can to avoid getting sucked into the wasteland. If you can advance straight from a successful mini-sale to proper contract negotiations, then do so. This can happen if you are not in a formal bidding process: once the prospect likes and trusts you, why shouldn't they sign you up?

If you are trapped in a formal process, conserve energy. Do everything you can to find out if you are a serious contender or just on a list to make up numbers. A previously successful mini-sale will help here: the person for whom you did a brilliant, albeit small, job, may be able to drop subtle hints.

Beauty parades

Ever seen the Miss World competition, where young women, in the spirit of world peace of course, march up and down catwalks to win prizes for their looks? You're just about to find out how they feel.

Beauty parades can take various forms, but all are variations on the theme of your being checked over by the potential client. They may send a team to visit you. Their Purchasing Director may meet your CEO. You may have to go and make a formal presentation to them, and have questions fired at you.

There are various hints for making the best of this irksome process:

Firstly, make the process as two-way as possible. What can you learn about them while this is going on?

Secondly, don't waste time and money on parades, unless you are a large company. Big companies often expect small ones to leap through endless hoops to gain their business. Yes, there is a possible big contract at the end of it, but I've seen small companies go broke pitching for big contracts.

Many beauty parades are faked: one of your fellow contestants has already been given the nod. Do as little bespoke work as possible for these events. As a small business you just don't have the resources.

Thirdly, at the parade, always try and match the client. Who will be representing them? The Finance Director? Bring your finance cornerstone along as well. A production manager? Bring your delivery cornerstone. Really smart teams in search of big orders match precisely: if there's going to be a secretary there taking notes, bring a secretary too. The purpose is to ensure that all conversations are carried out in the appropriate language – the rest of the human race don't speak finance-ese, however hard we try – and to create rapport between your organisations at as many levels as possible.

Actually, this principle of 'matching' is an excellent one for all relationships between businesses. If your receptionist knows their receptionist, their boss knows your boss (and so on), you are on a winner. Information can travel much faster and more efficiently across these networks than along the official ones of statements, press releases, formal complaints (etc).

Matching can work even if there is a great disparity in size between companies. If the sale is a routine one, then, no, there's no point in the boss of a start-up trying to become best mates with the CEO of BP. But if the sale is of something special, maybe your mentor knows the CEO and would be prepared to mention you when they next meet. 'I see you're thinking of buying some of those new grommets from Smartco…'

And at the same time, of course, the relevant technical people should get to know each other, and the entrepreneur should strike up an acquaintance with the head of the relevant department.

Note that if a lot of 'matching' is going on – and there should be – everybody has to understand the basic principles of closing. You never know when you are going to have to do a tiny piece of negotiation. Those principles are, you will recall, to work towards clear outcomes; to ask for those; to restate them once you think agreement has been reached; then to shut up. The sales cornerstone should be in charge of coaching the technical people, finance people and even the CEO in these basic skills.

Memo to all heads of sales: don't be afraid to assert your knowledge and authority on occasions like this. If the company has a financial issue, people turn to the CFO. This is a sales issue, and people should turn to you. If they don't, you are not being firm enough about your role in the company and its importance. Oddly enough, though most people slightly look down on sales, everyone thinks they can do it. They are wrong on both counts. But it is your responsibility, to yourself, to your company and to your profession, to disabuse people of these misconceptions.

Of course, matching is impossible for the sole trader or the tiny company. But you should have strategic allies who can help you out. If you're meeting an FD, bring your accountant. Maybe your mentor could accompany you.

As with any and every meeting, always aim for an outcome. A beauty parade may well end with a promise to contact you with a decision, or a comment like, 'We're drawing up a shortlist.' Pin them down for details of when this list will be announced, and who to contact if it is not announced by that time.

assert your
knowledge
and authority

Shortlists

It's nice to be on a shortlist: Chris's first cop novel was shortlisted for an international prize, and he's been sticking it in his publicity ever since. But it does nothing for cashflow. The opposite, actually: there will probably be more discussions and meetings, between technical people, financiers and so on, all of which consume valuable resources of time and money. However, it can boost morale, which is nice... until the bad news comes through. You came second.

If so, don't despair. It's not the end of the world. The company will probably come back to you another time. They certainly know who you are now, and you will have made contacts there which you should keep alive. Value and use these.

The deal

But sometimes the news is better. You've won! Ask the person for some formal notification – an email is fine.

Note that for small pieces of work you may never have a contract. In fact, I say you are usually better off without one. Lawyers will throw their hands up in horror at this, but anyone who's worked in a small business will know what I mean.

There is a lot to be said for the old-fashioned 'gentleman's agreement' (extended, of course, to gentlewomen). You and the customer have already mapped out a path towards a mutually beneficial, win-win outcome, so there is no real need to draw the map out again in legal-ese. And there is a danger in contracts: they invite people to call their lawyer first if things start going wrong, rather than call the person they should contact first – the other party. In *The Beermat Entrepreneur* I quoted the old maxim: 'Don't litigate, negotiate.' It remains profoundly true.

Also, if you make a gentleman's agreement and stick to it, you will begin to get the reputation of being someone who keeps their word, which is invaluable in business.

This does not mean 'be slapdash': make careful notes of what is agreed, and make sure both parties accept these as correct.

Of course, *larger* tranches of business will require a contract – in which case for heaven's sake get your lawyers to look through the thing. Yes, it will cost, but it is money well spent.

Whatever formal shape the agreement takes, it's time for a large (and very informal) celebration. Sports people are taught to celebrate success, which is why you see footballers hugging one another after a goal. No, you don't have to give the finance cornerstone a big sloppy kiss, but the team does need to have a special celebration.

The small-ticket business

As with information-gathering, the process I have described above will be different for the firm that has many, smaller clients. A two-person design company offering £1,000 websites can't even consider jumping through all these hoops. However the fundamental principles are the same. You must go through the stages up to the sanity check. For this check, get a headed-notepaper close. Your second meeting will be a kind of miniature beauty parade: you should be looking to close the sale.

If your business plans to sell small items direct to the consumer, you may consider this section of the book irrelevant. However, most such businesses end up dealing with intermediaries, such as retailers, at which point the process outlined above is exactly the one you need to follow.

For *all* businesses, a key to sales success is to speed up the sales process as much as possible. Whatever the size of the sale, no sole trader, start-up, SME or partnership can afford to have their time wasted.

Beyond the deal

Of course, the deal is not the end of the sales story. If there is a farmer account manager in the team, the hunter salesperson needs to hand over to them. (In the seedling start-up, the delivery cornerstone may well play the farmer role; the sole trader, of course, has to play both roles.)

The process of handing an account from hunter to farmer can be a tricky one. Rajiv got the initial business; suddenly Jane is introduced as the account manager. But the customer liked Rajiv; he's partly, or even largely, why you got the business in the first place. Hence Jane's need for sociability as well – farmers are never just administrators, but always 'cultivators of the relationship'. Part of the solution lies in having Rajiv still available to chat with the client. Jane may not like this, but she must accept it (and she must be told this will happen when she takes the job on). At the same time, Rajiv must accept that he now no longer has sole owner-ship of the relationship; he has become a kind of ambassador; he must report back to Jane what has been discussed in any chats with the customer and *she* must implement the solution.

Jane's job, at the most basic level, will be to keep in regular contact with the client. More business gets lost by neglect than by total incompetence, a fact I find amazing. 'They do a reasonable job, but we never see them,' is an oft-heard complaint – and music to the ears of a rival hunter. Clients like to be loved and reminded how important they are.

Beyond this, of course, there is a lot more. The farmer is a master listener. Few business arrangements – or any other human interaction for that matter – run totally smoothly, so small things will go wrong. These can turn into big things if not addressed. The good farmer has 'an ear for trouble', not in a negative sense, but simply objectively: they can spot when clients are less than delighted. Good farmers will then act on that perception, rather than just sweep it under the carpet. If 'always be closing' is the motto of the hunter, 'address issues quickly' should be that of the farmer.

the farmer
is a **master** listener

Late payment is an area where the farmer's skills are often needed. Initially this should be a finance matter. Many late payments are solved by a simple chat between accounts people, and should be solved like this. If this does not solve the problem, this is an issue that needs account manager attention.

A useful website with information on this topic is www.payontime.co.uk All kinds of solutions are discussed here. What matters to the farmer is to ensure that both they and the finance cornerstone understand the options, the company policy and that they agree on procedures.

Sole traders may so loathe chasing up cheques that they let late payers get away with it. Get your accountant (who is effectively your 'virtual finance cornerstone') to do this for you.

More on this topic in our forthcoming *Finance on a Beermat.*

The curse of late payers highlights the value of networking – not just with potential clients but with other players in your industry. In *The Beermat Entrepreneur* I talked about the right way to compete – hard but fair, as in sport, where you can have a drink with the oppo after a game (Jason Leonard is my model for this: one of the toughest props on the rugby field, he is known as a generous and friendly man in the clubhouse). During such a drink, conversation may well turn to customers in potential trouble or poor payers. If you trust the person you're talking with, this can be very useful information.

The farmer isn't just there to watch for problems, however. They are also on the lookout for *opportunities* – but I shall discuss this in the next chapter.

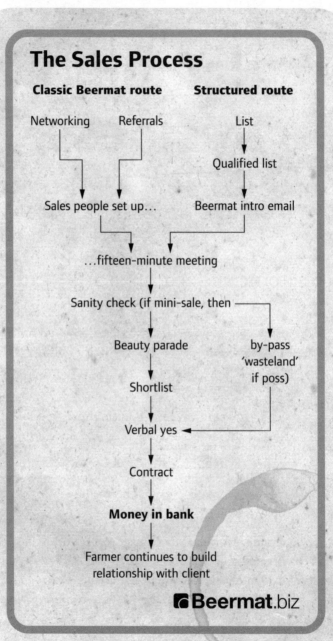

The Sales Process

Classic Beermat route **Structured route**

Networking   Referrals   List

Qualified list

Sales people set up…   Beermat intro email

…fifteen-minute meeting

Sanity check (if mini-sale, then

Beauty parade   by-pass 'wasteland' if poss)

Shortlist

Verbal yes

Contract

Money in bank

Farmer continues to build
relationship with client

Beermat.biz

Chapter 9: Ramping up Business

The methodology in the last chapter should ensure a regular supply of work. But how do you really hit the growth trail?

Farmers should be looking to grow business within the accounts they manage. It's their job to really get to know the organisation: all the people, all their issues, all the unexpressed needs that the busy hunter failed to notice.

How is this best done?

Don't overlook the obvious way: asking for more business. If you've done a great job in the area you agreed, just ask if there are any other areas where your key contact thinks you might be able to add value. Because you have proven your worth to the client, it is perfectly reasonable to ask: 'You spend £10,000 a year with us; what would you pay us £20,000 a year to do?' The answer is unlikely to be, 'X, and here's the money' – but it will get people thinking.

At the same time, ask your key contact to network you within the client organisation. If you are doing a great job for them, then they will probably be happy to do this – they will get kudos for introducing you, and the benefits you bring, around the place.

If you hear of a large slice of business potentially up for grabs in another part of the account company, it is time to send in the hunter. Talk it through first with your key contact. He or she will hopefully have fond memories of the hunter, and will be happy to see them sent into another part of the company.

For the hunter, the key to ramping up business is simple: do more selling. There is a 'numbers' element to sales – the more calls you make, the more you will sell (provided the calls are done properly and not shoddily, cutting corners to boost a rigid 'number of calls made' metric). It's the old Gary Player thing I quoted at the start of *Beermat* – 'The harder I practice, the luckier I get.'

The easiest way for a business to make more calls is to get more salespeople. In the start-up, this creates an interesting situation for the sales cornerstone, who was originally the only hunter in the company. Soon after, a couple of farmers arrived, to managed the accounts he or she had so successfully won. Now other hunters are appearing, and the cornerstone is in danger of being promoted to sales manager.

As I said, I don't enjoy doing sales management, and most hunters are the same. However it must be done, and there is a magical device to make the job easier – the Beermat Sales Pipeline. This tool, of course, is not just for start-ups. Every business should have, and swear by, one of these. An amazing number don't.

The Beermat Sales Pipeline builds on the narrative of the last chapter. A sale is *process*, not a one-off event, and you monitor its progress by seeing whether it has passed certain markers or not. Passing each marker makes the eventual arrival of the cheque more likely, so you can attach numerical probabilities to each stage. Multiply these by the expected value of the cheque, and you have a 'pipeline value' for the deal. Add these up, and you have a 'total pipeline value'.

Using the diagram at the end of the last chapter, let's break the progress of a sale into ten stages.

Stage One: the prospect is on a list

Stage Two: the prospect is on a properly qualified list (information, not just data)

Stage Three: a fifteen-minute meeting has been arranged

Stage Four: they are a *serious* prospect: they have needs and the money to pay for your solution to those needs, right now

Stage Five: they pass at least one sanity check

Stage Six: a 'beauty parade' happens

Stage Seven: you are on the shortlist

Stage Eight: you get a verbal yes

Stage Nine: the contract is signed

Stage Ten: the money is in the bank

Clearly some sales leap a stage or two. This is essentially a model of a largish sale: for a small sale like a one-off website for a small trader, Stage Six would be your second meeting, and you would be pushing for a verbal yes at that meeting. Classic Beermat sales leapfrog the early stages: you meet someone at a networking event; you get on and pencil in a business meeting there and then (or even – I've known it happen – they say, 'as a matter of fact, we're looking to buy one of those right now'; at which point the sale has leapt straight to Stage Four).

Other times, of course, the sales process can get bogged down, especially in the 'wasteland' between Stages Six and Nine.

Tweak the pipeline to fit your business. There may, for example, be a series of steps set by customers whereby you sell them things for a while, then get on to a formal list of suppliers (or get to become an exclusive supplier). Reflect this in the middle stages of the model: the opening stages of qualifying are pretty invariant, as are the closing ones of actually signing and delivering.

This isn't just for large businesses. An aromatherapist operating her own business should be using both the Beermat networking/referrals approach and the structured 'list' approach to generate leads. Fifteen-minute meetings are probably not time-effective, so make Stage Four a phone call where the outcome is a verbal yes for a trial session. That session is a sanity check (Stage Five). When the customer says: 'That was great, I'll have the full course of sessions you talked about,' leap up to Stage Eight. If you charge in advance, ask for the money straight away, and get it, you have shot straight to that perfect Ten!

Note that this is a hunter's model, ending as it does when the first cheque arrives. Farmers know that the long-term selling job has just begun…but in order to ramp up sales effectively, you must have hunters out there seeking new business.

To turn this model into a better predictive mechanism, I turn the stages into decimals, so that stage 1 becomes 0.1, stage 2 becomes 0.2 (all the way up to 1.0). The list is restated below:

0.1: the prospect is on a list

0.2: the prospect is on a properly qualified list

0.3: a fifteen-minute meeting has been arranged

0.4: they are a *serious* prospect: they have needs and the money to pay for your solution to those needs, right now

0.5: they pass a sanity check

0.6: a 'beauty parade' happens

0.7: you are on the shortlist

0.8:   you get a verbal yes

0.9:   you get a formal yes

1.0:   the money is in the bank

Note that there is a kind of 'sub-routine' at 0.5: the progress of a mini-sale can be followed through:

★ Small job agreed

★ Start date agreed

★ Job done

★ Job assessed

Every salesperson should know exactly where each one of the sales they are pursuing is on the big scale. So should their manager.

The information has three key uses: to stop sales getting bogged down, to estimate future revenue streams and to estimate future workloads.

Keeping sales moving. Every month the sales manager meets with the salespeople – one to one – and runs through their list of progressing sales. If any of these sales has not moved up the scale, the salesperson must have an explanation why. There's usually a reasonable one, for a while. But if the sale refuses to move along the pipeline, the sales manager should remove it from the list. 'Let's face it, nothing's happening with Amalgamated Grommets. You're better off spending time elsewhere…'

This isn't the same as forbidding the salesperson to keep the sale going, if they really think it will work in the end. But it's no longer on the formal list by which the salesperson's work is assessed, and will have to make progress to reappear.

In practice, pay little attention to 0.1 and 0.2. Only at 0.3 can one use the word 'prospect' in a meaningful sense.

Predicting cashflow. Especially in start–ups, but also in many SMEs where income is not regular, predicting cashflow is notoriously difficult. It is also very important – more established businesses go broke from cashflow problems than from any other cause.

The Beermat Sales Pipeline will produce an income estimate. Yes, it is a very conservative one, especially a few months out, but once the system has been running for a while, the figures can be interpreted. 'Usually our Beermat Revenue Forecast is £35,000 – this month we're looking at £17,000,' is very useful information.

The technique is simple: multiply the status of the sale by your best estimate of its expected yield to get a figure for this. A simple example… You have four sales on the go. One is a contract for £15,000, at stage 0.4. Another is a smaller contract for £9,000, which you have been told is yours but no paperwork is done. Tomorrow you are going into a beauty parade for a contract worth £20,000. And your hunter has set up a fifteen-minute meeting for a contract that could bring in £100,000.

Your revenue prediction sheet will look like this:

Customer	Stage of Sale		Expected value (£)	'Beermat' value (£)
United Grommets	0.4	×	15,000	6,000
Borough of Neasden	0.8	×	9,000	7,200
Amalgamated Fittings	0.6	×	20,000	12,000
'Beermat' Revenue Forecast				25,200

Note that the nice juicy £100,000 contract isn't there. You can't put it on the Beermat Sales Forecast until you get to 0.4, until they are a serious prospect with needs and money right now.

Cautious sales managers will then divide the Beermat expected revenue by two, because it's a hard world and salespeople have been known to be over-optimistic about the chances of success. This produces a conservative Beermat Revenue Forecast of £12,600.

Yes, you will hope to exceed this – but the BRF can be measured month-on-month and will reveal trends.

For start-ups, or any business that has yet to establish a regular revenue pattern, I don't see any harm in using the Beermat Revenue Forecast as an estimate of future income. It's as reliable as anything else, and will keep people on their toes. What revenue targets has the CEO set, and does the forecast match them?

A third use is to forecast **levels of future work**. The delivery cornerstone should be watching the pipeline like a hawk, too. Can we really can support these sales?

After a while, companies with lots of sales will recognise a regular shape to the pipeline. Note the value of each stage. If there's an unusual 'bulge' in the middle, deals are not being closed. If the middle is looking thinner than normal, more effort needs to be made on creating new leads and following them up.

Note that when you start using the Beermat Sales Pipeline, you get a strange dip in the sales forecast in the first few iterations. This is because salespeople were excessively optimistic when the table was first drawn up. In the few months after that, the unlikely sales drop off the list. After that, however, things pick up, as the new discipline gets the sales force moving sales through the system quicker.

Of course, like all business tools, the pipeline has to be used properly. Keep it up to date; press the salespeople on the position of their sales every fortnight; make sure everyone senior person in the business – or why not everybody in the business? – knows the Beermat Revenue Forecast.

The Beermat strategic seminar

This is a powerful way of getting new prospects, and of turning a few of them into serious prospects very quickly. If done well, it is also fun.

It is particularly useful for high-tech companies, where the technology and its potential will be of general interest. We used it regularly at The Instruction Set, as there was a buzz about UNIX, and it bought us loads of business.

Organise a seminar on the subject of practical applications of the technology in which you specialise. Ask customers to speak at it, to tell their story of how using your technology solved pain for them. You might get a technical expert to give one of the talks, but watch out that what they say doesn't go over people's heads and bore them. Your own role? Onstage, virtually nothing. You welcome people, explain where the loos, coffee and lunch are, introduce the speakers then shut up. At no point do you try and sell anything.

At the same time, of course, you have your salespeople working the room – again, not doing any selling, but talking to people and listening to their stories. (OK, they are doing sales work, but they are qualifying not closing.) Be ruthless about this. Task each one with meeting ten people – give them the names in advance. Afterwards debrief them about the stories they have heard. Any buying signals? Any other market information?

The seminar should be for the morning only. Have a free buffet lunch (don't bother with a sit-down, they cost a lot more but are rarely that much nicer), available from 12.30 onwards for people who want to stay and chat – a nice automatic selection mechanism. Also, have a demo of your product in a back room somewhere, and invite 'anyone who's interested' to come and have a play with it. Usually these will be the ones with a real commercial interest. I've taken orders from people at these back-room demos.

We used to run our seminars in Central London on a Friday. Many people from the regions came down to London and 'made a weekend of it': London-based customers tended to hover over lunch then say, 'There's no point in going back to the office now, is there?'

Aim for a hundred guests. That way there are enough people there to make the thing feel like a serious event, but plenty of room for people to move around and nobody should be forced to stand or sit where they can't hear the speakers.

Always charge. If nobody will pay for the seminar, then you have to wonder if your technology is as interesting as you think. At The Instruction Set, we never had any problems filling venues – it's not as if executives of large companies are paying out of their own pockets – and the fact of charging cuts down the no-shows radically.

Make sure you get the venue right. What are the acoustics like? Does the PA work? (Do they have special microphones that can only pick up a voice if you stand a millimetre away? Does the system erupt into an impression of a Jimi Hendrix guitar solo the moment anyone turns the volume above two?) Does the heating/air conditioning work? (I remember sweltering through a conference for venture capitalists at a supposedly posh London venue which had no air conditioning. I guess it was preparing some of the VCs for their next life, but I didn't enjoy the experience.) What are the staff like? Some hotels seem to employ gloomy, and no doubt appallingly-paid, people who make Dostoevsky look like Ronald McDonald. How accessible is the venue? Some parts of 'Central London' are an awfully long way from Tube stations.

With the right venue, you feel good the moment you walk in, and it stays that way till you leave.

As with all sales efforts, follow up assiduously. Once you have debriefed your people about the guests they spoke to, you should compose an individual, personal email to each one. Some of these can be generic. If the guest expressed no great interest and left as soon as they could, simply thank them for turning up and ask what they found most interesting about the occasion. But with anyone who sent out anything remotely resembling a buying signal, take much more care. What interested them? Did they say or hint where their 'pain' was? Be systematic; be thorough.

If it is done well, the strategic seminar can fill a sales pipeline with prospects, at several stages, at a fraction of the cost of a hundred sales visits.

follow up
assiduously

Market communication in the twenty-first century

You need to be telling the world about what you do, but I am very sceptical of a lot of marketing and PR that goes on.

I particularly hate *brochures*. I think it's dreadful the way that 'business advisors' tell start-ups to spend valuable seed capital on these expensive and useless distractions.

Brochures are ways of ducking out of closing. How many sales have been lost by so-called salespeople meeting buying signals and customer interest with…a brochure? Even if we've never been in this position, we all know what it's like to hide behind a brochure. When someone phones us trying to sell kitchens or utilities, and we're in a nice mood so don't want to tell them to **★★★★** off, what do we say? 'Send me a brochure.'

Secondly, start-ups often aren't quite sure what they are selling. Once the business is up and running, you will know exactly what the customer pain is and why you are the best people in the world to solve it. Until then, it is easy to fall into the trap of having a brochure printed too early, then finding that nobody wants what's on pages three to six: the stuff on page seven 'has the magic' (and even then, you have decided to offer it in a slightly different way since the brochure was printed…).

If you must have some kind of brochure – put it up on the web, where it is easier to change.

Another reason for avoiding brochures is that they cost a lot of money. Simple as that.

Oh, and brochures always get argued about. 'It should be blue!' 'No, yellow!' You have better things to do.

Should you ever have a brochure?

I accept that for some direct-to-consumer businesses, especially ones with strong local appeal, some kind of flyer or handout is necessary. But keep them cheap and cheerful.

For other businesses, consider having a Beermat Brochure, once you are clear about your product, how you are going to sell it and to whom. Actually, this isn't a brochure at all, but a series of case studies.

If I were joining a company tomorrow, the first thing I would do is get them to write up case studies of different types of customer they have helped. Each one would tell a story. Like all good stories, change took place: the customer was in pain at the start of the story and happy at the end, thanks to our intervention. For any given prospect, they would receive the case history that most resembles their own issue. 'We helped someone like you the other day. Here's what happened.'

Obviously you have to clear it with the customer whose story you wish to tell. They may insist you hide their identity, which is fine – though best of all if they don't – and agree to act as referees, whom the prospect can phone and chat to about the story.

Beermat.biz

I mentioned *websites* above. These are really much more use than brochures. The start-up should have a very simple site: the company name, elevator pitch and phone number will do for Day One. But develop the site as the business grows.

Some hints:

★ Avoid expensive technology: most potential customers will be logging on via ordinary machines. My pet hate is flash: if I want to watch a movie, I'll go to the cinema; when I log on, it is in search of information

★ Don't have endless pictures of chairmen, smart offices etc. People don't care. Do list the names of your people, plus small pictures so people logging on can say, 'Yes, that is the bloke I met at that networking event the other week...'

★ Do put on lots of happy customer stories. Also any 'thought leadership' pieces by your people

★ Make it easy for people to contact you back

★ If you can capture email addresses, that's good, but make sure that the capture mechanism doesn't annoy the client. Make them enter a competition with a prize worth winning. My personal hate is electronic forms that don't work, which you spend valuable time filling in and get rewarded by a box telling you that you haven't filled it in properly

★ Do get a professional designer to do the work. People very quickly exit from sites they don't like

★ Do have a clear, accurate, simple-to-download map available for anyone coming to visit your premises

If you can sell *direct* over the Internet, do so. Such selling, which is usually of smallish consumer items (think Amazon), is not really the subject of this book. The Beermat approach, of adding service wherever possible, militates against direct, via-the-Internet selling: the medium is too impersonal.

You might be able to sell a few places on a training course through the net – 'book here!' – but you will never sell a training programme to a big customer.

Traditional printed *newsletters* suffer from the same problem as brochures – they cost a lot to produce; most people bin them; worst of all, they become an excuse for not making personal contact with people.

A cheap, online newsletter you write yourself is a much better idea. It doesn't have to have a fancy format: an ordinary email will do fine. Remember that its main job is as a 'nudge' to people in your network to remind them you are around and on the ball. As such, it is a part of your networking strategy, not a substitute for networking in person.

Advertising is usually wasteful, unless your differentiator is 'local' and you can advertise in cheap local media, or you are selling into a niche neatly covered by a specialist publication (but in that case, try and get free PR instead).

So is a lot of *PR*. To be fair to PR, it is up to a point a victim of its own success. It is so pervasive nowadays that consumers have become wary.

That said, some practitioners could try and use a little more imagination. I have done work with some brilliant PR people, who are usually very aware of the limited magic they can weave, but I have also seen dreadful PR. So many press releases are still unimaginably dull, and so many stunts embarrassingly obvious. I was once talked into getting a PR agency to rustle up some famous people for a charity gig I was running. They gave me a splendid-sounding list, of which not a single person actually turned up, then had the nerve to ask me for money.

The problem with PR, of course, is that it's engineered. This is particularly true of celebrity endorsements. Everyone knows that such-and-such a famous footballer doesn't drink such-and-such a soft drink, they just get paid to sit there grinning with a bottle of it in their hand. The only kind of endorsement that people take seriously is personal. The best is word of mouth.

In this environment, what can you do to get the word spread about your product?

The key to success is getting the right people to do it for you. Not Z-list celebrities, but people whose word counts in the community. In his excellent book *The Tipping Point*, Malcolm Gladwell talks about three key allies: connectors, mavens and persuaders. All of these should become evangelists for your product.

Connectors are the master networkers, like Carole Stone whom I mentioned in Chapter Two. They take pride in the size of their address book, not in a snobbish way, but because they view meeting and getting to know new people as a joy and an achievement. They often have an amazing memory for faces and for details of people's lives. They have a capacity for interest in people which extends across all boundaries (most of us socialise with people like ourselves). What you need from connectors is for them to like your product – then watch the news get round their network.

Mavens are less gregarious than connectors. Their great skill is knowing a lot about a small area. If there's a person you turn to when you want to know all about widgets, that person is a maven. Mavens may well be the sort of people who join trade associations or write pieces for the trade press. There are also 'consumer mavens' who go round telling people how to get the best deal on cars, phones (etc). In all cases, mavens do what they do (is there a verb, to mave?) from pleasure, for love of the research, and for the status and nice feelings that come from being consulted by other people and regarded by them as an expert.

Connectors, of course, need information to keep their networks 'buzzing', so will naturally gravitate towards mavens – who in turn will enjoy the recognition this brings.

Persuaders are people with 'the gift of the gab', people who are just naturally good at persuading people to do things. They are the sales naturals, the social magnets, with that charm I talked about in Chapter One, that natural ability to put people at ease and establish rapport.

Note, I am not talking about people you employ here. Your salespeople must have persuader charm and be good net-workers, but this section isn't about them. It's about people in the world out there, whom you need to get 'on your side' and telling the world about what you do – not because you pay them but because they want to.

How do you find and motivate these external evangelists?

It is essential to start with a great product. Yes, this is obvious, but none of this works with a substandard product. So make sure you have a differentiator and deliver superbly.

If you know of any people like this in your community, see if you can get someone to network you with them, and offer them a free sample. Don't force the issue, however: people like this don't like being pressurised.

Always encourage happy clients to tell their friends. In practice what will happen is that some of these clients will be natural persuaders, who will bring in a stream of prospects, eager to buy (or at least to try). Some will be natural connectors, who will create a flow of interest: their contacts will probably need a little more selling to. Mavens will be more critical: work hard to win them over.

Once you have evangelists, reward them. If they are bringing you business, give them stuff cheap. Treat them to a special customer event. For a big firm this can be something lavish. For a sole trader operating on a tight budget, use your imagination. If nothing else, invite them round for dinner. For mavens, organise a talk by an expert on the subject.

Don't forget the other, more traditional forms of *free PR*. A one-person business may not be able to get a hundred people to a strategic seminar, but there are all sorts of small organisations looking for speakers. Chris used to chair the Civic Society in Baldock, and they had monthly evenings when people came to talk about all kinds of things from the life-cycle of the crested grebe to the Battle of Trafalgar. Develop a short talk or demonstration based around what you do, and offer it locally. People are always interested in what other people do for a living.

Can you write pieces for local papers? Once you build up a backlog of experience, ask yourself what was your most interesting piece of work: would it make a case study for that wonderfully diverse trade press? We write a regular piece for the Institute of Directors' magazine; there's always something to say each month.

Finally, can you gain access to a *network?* I am often approached by people wanting to email the Beermat network. I usually say no as I value my network, and one easy way to break it up is to overuse it, especially by firing off ads for stuff I don't know much about. But if the person can make a really strong case that they have something that will benefit a reasonable proportion of my network, then I'll at least mention them in a mailout.

After that, the 'network effect' should take over, with people in the network telling each other how they found this fantastic widget that saved them £1,000. If it does not, then have another look at the product.

Getting access to a network is basically a kind of strategic alliance, and as in all such alliances, the outcome must be a win-win – or in this case, a win-win-win: the person applying gets exposure; the people in the network get information about something that is of real use to them; the network 'node' or owner gets cred for having facilitated this information transfer.

always **encourage** happy clients to **tell** their friends

Strategic alliances

These are important for Beermat businesses in all sorts of ways. Here I will just talk about how they can ramp up your sales.

Cross-referral is an obvious but useful method. If you are a sole trader offering one type of benefit, can you do a deal with other people who offer complementary benefits? For example, householders need a range of services: plumbers, electricians, carpenters, decorators etc. They also tend to worry about quality: who better to ask who would do a good job at X than someone who has done a good job in area Y?

The catch here is, of course, that the person you recommend has to be as good as you. So you may have to turn down people who ask to be recommended: indeed you have to be ruthless about this. Be totally objective about the person, and recommend them only if they are up to your own standard of excellence. If anyone asks you to recommend them, make it clear that you only do so under special circumstances. That way they'll be delighted if you do, and less disappointed if you don't.

If someone asks for a recommendation, don't give one unless you know your stuff. Do you know a subject maven? Network the enquirer with them...

If you earn a lot of your money from sub-contracted work, you may be asked to become a 'preferred supplier'. This is a kind of strategic alliance, but not nearly as fruitful in my view as the more informal alliances of equals above. Often this is just a way big companies can appear to look good – 'look at all the small businesses we're helping' – while in fact they are selling you training you don't really need and can hardly afford, and making you waste time jumping through hoops. Promised sales leads fail to materialise, and the whole thing turns out to have been a waste of time and money.

The only time I would recommend this is if you have a specific person in the organisation whom you like and trust – in other words, a customer mentor – who will definitely give you business if you get the official seal of approval. (In theory, the procedure also might be worth going through if the training were so brilliant that it really changed your company, but I have not found any evidence of this. The best training is provided via professional trainers in the competitive marketplace, not from big companies protected from competition by their size.)

Please don't for a moment fall for the old one about how having 'Official Megacorp Supplier' on your notepaper will impress anyone else. If it's the only way you can sell them anything, and they really will buy from you, then it is a necessity. But that's all it is. Such endorsements are about as useful as 'Official Supplier of Toilet Paper to the 1985 European Tiddlywinks Championships'.

What matters, of course, is having a good relationship with individual people at Megacorp.

The best strategic alliances are based on trust and personal rapport. This is true for relationships between small businesses, and relationships between small businesses and big ones. However attractive an alliance may look on paper, if you don't like your key contact, walk away. It won't work, and the prospective benefits won't accrue.

In alliances between small and large companies, things can go wrong if a key contact is moved to a new job. There's no real remedy for this; that's a risk of dealing with big business. If you really liked the old contact, talk them through what's happening – maybe they can suggest a way forward. However, don't let this put you off forming alliances, especially informal ones, with big companies. Yes, they might disappear, but they probably won't, and while they are around they are hugely useful.

Channels = conflict

There are various kinds of agencies, distributors and so on who will offer to do your selling for you. Unsurprisingly, I am dead against these. Two main reasons: firstly there is always *channel conflict*. Any intermediary's loyalty is split. Yes, their loyalty is partly to you, but it is also partly to their customers, and partly to all the other people they represent. In a conflict situation they will take whichever side suits them – and one can hardly blame them for that. If faced with a choice between upsetting Exxon or you, Fred Bloggs Widgets of Wythenshawe, guess which option they will choose.

Naturally, they will never admit to this fact!

Secondly there is the *chain of communication*. Beermat sales isn't just about flogging things to people. It's about building relationships between yourself and key customers. It's about constantly evolving the product in response to those customers' needs. At the start of the product's life, this evolution can be very fast: if the customer is unhappy you need to know why, in full detail, at once. Once the product has settled into its best possible form – or several forms if different ones suit different markets – evolution will still be on going. Customer needs will be perennially changing, and *you* need to be perpetually asking how you can help them meet these needs. I stress 'you', not someone acting on behalf of you and on behalf of a load of other people too.

Modern information theory has plenty to say on the deterioration of the quality of information as chains of communication get longer. If you haven't got time to read up on this topic, have a quick game of 'Chinese whispers' with a few friends, preferably after a drink or two: that will be a lot more fun and will make the point just as well.

The need to get 'closer to customers' is even felt by companies who mass-produce consumer goods. They are experimenting with ways of using the Internet to get one-to-one relationships with the people who buy their stuff in the shops. I'm not sure it will work – I have enough to think about in life, without worrying about my relationship with a can of baked beans – but I fully understand the motivation. The taking on of inter-mediaries is a step in the opposite direction.

Can intermediaries ever add value? I guess if all of the following are true:

★ you are a sole trader or very small business

★ you know a particular agent well

★ you like and trust them

★ they like and trust you

★ you respect their knowledge of a specialist (and rather complicated) market…

★ …about which you know rather little

Authors, actually, fall into this category: Chris and I have a very good agent! But if any of the above does not apply, there are better ways of selling.

I have been horrified by stories I have met from entrepreneurs (and particularly inventors) who have paid money to marketing agents to promote their product and got nothing back, except demands for more money to do more marketing.

If you are planning to enter a foreign market, do so with care. Many good companies have foundered trying to globalise what was actually a national product. In theory agents ought to help here, but in practice I suggest talking to local businesses until you find one you really like and respect, then work on a strategic alliance with them.

There are also legal issues about getting representation in Europe: current EU law means that people can claim to have been appointed 'your agent' on very flimsy grounds. Best not even enter into conversations on this topic.

All round the world, sales are ultimately about human relationships. Remember that motto: *people buy from people*.

Ramping up sales – on a Beermat

★ **Increase activity levels**

- more sales people

- cut sales cycle

- always be closing!

★ **Monitor**

- Beermat Sales Pipeline

★ **Beermat Strategic Seminar**

★ **Evangelists**

- connectors, mavens and persuaders

- among customers and staff

★ **Strategic alliances**

- based on personality not theory

★ **Avoid agents / distributors**

- except in very specific circumstances

Beermat.biz

Chapter 10: **And Finally...**

It is an essential part of the Beermat philosophy that business should be fun. Not a riot all the time, but exciting, engrossing, challenging and human. Nowhere is this more the case than in sales, which is why my heart sinks every time I get a bored voice on a phone reading me a script about phone charges or replacement windows.

Selling is about being yourself, not about lying. If you a natural 'people person', then it should be an enjoyable experience. If you are shyer, then accept the fact and play the biggest role in the sales process you can, even if it's only evangelising the product among old friends.

Everybody in a vibrant, dynamic business sells. Everybody can and should enjoy the process.

business should be fun

I hope this book has got that message across to you. If it has, take it further – make sales training part of your general business education. For yourself, and, if you are in a position to do so, for the people for whom you are responsible.

If, as part of that business education, you end up at a business school, and you're on an entrepreneurship module, and Chris or I come and talk to you and ask, as we will, if you've done sales training – raise your hand with pride. It shows you really want to understand the heartbeat of business, not just the latest management fad.

Good luck, and enjoy the journey.

Appendix A: Sales in a Professional Partnership

Success for professional partnerships is becoming more and more about sales. This is seen by some as a 'dumbing-down'. Not surprisingly, I disagree. It is actually a compliment to the profession: excellence of delivery has now become standard, so a new differentiator is needed. By making this differentiator sales, a partnership is ensuring that it stays close to its customers and responsive to their needs, not as a theoretical notion or a slogan, but as a working, day-to-day reality.

However, the arrival of a sales ethos in a professional partnership needs to be handled correctly. A first step is often to appoint someone 'marketing partner'. This is already two, maybe three, mistakes. Mistake number one, of course, is calling it marketing not sales, thereby buying into an old snobbery and dishonesty. Their job may well have a marketing aspect to it – the strategic assessment of what niches in the overall market the partnership serves. But once this assessment has been made, the job is a sales one, communicating *in person* with the key individuals in those niches. Especially in the world of professional services, that old adage is true: *people buy from people.*

The second mistake is to appoint one person to do this job. This will send the message that, 'Joanna has taken the marketing job, so that's that sorted, and the rest of us can get back to doing exactly what we did before.' No. Everybody from now on sells!

A common third mistake will lie in appointing the wrong person to this job: someone who finds the abstract, intellectual challenge of marketing interesting, but who lacks the sales personality.

The Beermat approach avoids these three mistakes.

Step one is to make the strategic, marketer's decision about the part of the market you will serve. This must be made by the top team (or, if there is such a person, by the natural leader of the partnership, the person who would be the charismatic CEO if you were a PLC – but we much prefer the team approach!) In many long-standing partnerships the market will already be understood. It would be sensible for the top team to have a think about exactly *how well* the market is understood – and even more sensible to have a workshop day where everyone in the partnership, including the post-boy, is invited to consider the nature of the market – but don't do too much navel-gazing. If you are a new partnership, remember Goldman's Law – 'Nobody knows anything' – and make this strategic decision provisional. The market may start screaming at you to change (if it does, you will hear the scream via your sales initiatives).

The second step is to divide your people into salespeople and non-salespeople. Who are the 'clubbable', sociable networkers, and who are the quiet ones who deliver well but lack that personal magic? Be honest, as most people will like to see themselves as the former. Try and make clear that there is no stigma attached to being the latter – it takes a range of character types to create a great business: one that was nothing but extroverts would probably amass orders then fail to deliver; a team of introverts will be capable of brilliant work but not get any.

Your sales naturals should all be tasked with selling.

The third step is to appoint a professional sales manager to manage the sales process. This is essential because without such a person staring at the Beermat Sales Pipeline every day and nagging the sales naturals to move their prospects along it, the sales process will bog down. Note that experience in the professional sector is not essential for this job. A small partnership could consider outsourcing this and have a part-timer come in, say, two days a week. Don't appoint someone who doesn't understand sales to do this job.

A fourth step is to provide training for everyone. The sales naturals need sales training; the quiet ones need to know how to network among their peers, gather information and pass that information on to the sales manager.

The organisation will soon be sales-focused without actually having made huge changes to how its staff behave. The sales naturals will be better at following up the leads they come across; the quiet ones will be better at handing over prospects to a sales team. The main differences should be that customers will seem to matter more – oh, and you should make a lot more money.

Appendix B: Sales for the Sole Trader

Many of the people I teach are not planning to found business empires: they just have a skill and want to earn a living out of it, working for themselves as consultants, life coaches, plumbers, freelance journalists (and so on – the list, in the modern world, is endless). They have discovered that in order to do this, they have to sell.

This is usually a painful discovery.

The same goes for franchisees, who often think they are 'buying a job' via a franchise. They are not. They are buying a business. They will get some marketing support from the franchisor, but in many of these operations, Beermat sales skills can make the difference between success and failure. People who are diffident about selling should be very cautious about taking up franchises. Sales naturals should consider this option very seriously – if you like the sound of the business, and think it will mean selling to people whom you will, by and large, like, then you could be on to a winner.

Entrepreneurs need cornerstones to provide essential perspective and breadth of expertise in finance, delivery and sales. As a one-person business, you face exactly the same need to cover these bases, but face the need on your own. You can't hire the expertise in full-time. You either have to do it yourself or get some part-time assistance.

The latter option is often taken regarding *finance*: most sole traders have someone who comes in regularly to 'do the books'.

Delivery is usually the easy, enjoyable bit. Many sole traders are people with a skill, be it woodturning or reflexology: the business is a means to refine and profit from this skill. Because they love it and are good at it, they deliver it superbly.

Selling is what most one-person businesses do worst. Why? Because the kind of character that makes a great craftsperson usually makes a poor salesperson. This is very bad news, as Emerson's famous aphorism that if you make a better mousetrap, the world will 'make a beaten path to your door', is just plain wrong. You'll just sit at home all day twiddling with refinements to the mousetrap, writing angry letters to *Mousetrap World* (incorporating *Rodent Capture Weekly*) and getting into debt. But you can't hire salespeople in the way you can an accountant. What is to be done?

The answer is, of course, that you have to do the selling yourself. All of it.

★ You must research

★ You must network – and if you are painfully shy, you must *make* yourself network. You can do some of this online, but in the end you need to get out there and meet people

★ You must follow up networking contacts with brief, focused 'hunter' phone calls where the object is to get a brief meeting

★ At that meeting, you must close. Yes, you'll be asking for money! This is really tough. Even sales cornerstones are asking for money on behalf of a business (even if it's only them and a couple of mates): you are asking for yourself, and yourself only. The trick is to use 'script and silence' (see page 44)

★ You must look out for ways of getting free or cheap publicity (see page 133)

★ You must cultivate your favourite clients and incentivise them to act as 'evangelists' for you

★ You must manage your own Beermat Sales Pipeline, and be firm with yourself if the pipeline starts to run dry

★ You must have a simple, attractive, informative website

★ You must be on the lookout for good strategic allies, for example people in complementary areas with whom you can cross-refer clients (see page 134)

★ You can extend this notion, and actually team up with other people. Many partnerships begin as a loose confederation of solo experts who work together for psychological support as well as for business reasons, and find they do more and more stuff as a team. I work with a group of speakers who operate in this way. United Artists started like this, too, as did the Magnum photographers' agency

You do not have the option of doing nothing about sales.

There are almost no business people who love finance, sales *and* delivery with equal passion. You're lucky if you love one, 'don't mind' another and can just tolerate the third. But you must spend time on all three – despite the endless temptations to do more of the bit you like and to put off doing the stuff you hate. This temptation is powerful, not just because the one you like is more fun, but because there will be a voice in the back of your head saying that the other stuff doesn't really matter: 'The mousetraps are going to make me rich, so adding another feature is time well spent – just wait till the customers start pouring in…'

They won't come pouring in. Unless you sell to them.

The good news is that you can come to enjoy sales, if you follow the advice in this book. No, the asking for money bit probably won't be fun – but make a challenge out of it. Remember the old adage, 'Who dares, wins.'

In the end, your sales efforts will enable you to do what you set out to do when you 'went solo' – to practice your skills and get paid a decent wage for it. Think of this as you plough through lists of contacts or look at a list of calls you have to make: it's the price of sustainable freedom.

Appendix C: **Sales Cornerstones and Entrepreneurs**

Entrepreneurs, and no doubt some bosses of SMEs, senior partners etc, think they can sell. They usually can't. They can do some aspects of selling brilliantly, but not the whole thing. If you look back at the list of sales attributes, the reason will become clear.

Above all, sales people have to be liked. Most entrepreneurs are pretty good at this, having charm aplenty. But some are not – and still think they can sell, probably because they can bully people inside their organisations and think they can do the same to the world outside. They can't.

But salespeople also need to be good listeners. Entrepreneurs are usually incredibly poor listeners. They are far too focused on their own ideas and projects. This is a good thing; they have an agenda and intend driving it though, and this is necessary for the survival of the business. But it does not make for good sales.

They often lack real empathy with others – again, a good thing, as their job is to envisage great things and make them happen, not to 'be nice to everybody'.

Entrepreneurs are often impatient: salespeople have to be patient. And they can lack focus, while salespeople must focus all the time.

The wise sales cornerstone uses the best aspects of the entrepreneur to energise sales sessions by stage-managing their appearance. Especially at a beauty parade, it is great to wheel the entrepreneur in to give a brief, passionate description of the business and why it is special – then have them hurry off to do other stuff while you do the rest of the selling.

Because sales 'looks easy' to entrepreneurs – who have some of the sales virtues but not all – sales cornerstones often need to defend their independence against entrepreneurial encroachment. I once had a boss retarget all my sales force, without telling me (I resigned shortly after). Other bosses have suddenly decided to phone up my customers and do a bit of negotiation.

This really isn't on – but it is up the sales cornerstone to make that clear. You are a professional; most entrepreneurs are (often very) gifted amateurs.

In the end, it comes down to pride in your profession. I hope this book has helped give you that. Your work should build your pride further, with every satisfied customer.